LI'L ABNER

Dailies
Volume Eight: 1942

Al Capp

KITCHEN SINK PRESS

Princeton Wisconsin

ISBN 0-87816-068-X (hardcover)
ISBN 0-87816-069-8 (softcover)

This is the eighth volume of the complete *Al Capp's Li'l Abner*, reprinting the 1942 daily strip. The series is published by Kitchen Sink Press, **Denis Kitchen**, publisher. The series editor is **Dave Schreiner**. The cover was designed and colored by art director **Ray Fehrenbach**, who, with **Christi Scholl**, retouched and assembled the strips for publication. Final proofreading was done by **Doreen Riley.** We wish to thank members of the Capp estate for their cooperation in publishing this series, **Maurice Horn** for his introduction, and **Bill Blackbeard** of the San Francisco Academy of Comic Art for supplying us with the few missing strips we needed to complete this volume.

Library of Congress Cataloging-in-Publication Data

Capp, Al, 1909-
    Li'l Abner : dailies.

    Includes index.
    Contents: v. 8. 1942
    I. Title.
PN6728.L5C29   1988   741.5'973   88-12831
ISBN 0-87816-068-X (v. 8)
ISBN 0-87816-069-8 (pbk. : v. 8)

Li'l Abner in wartime: the mystery of the dog that didn't bark in the night

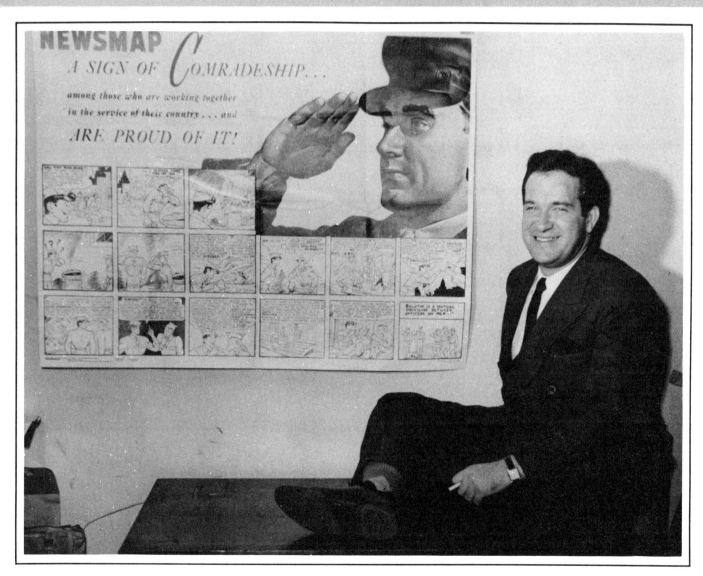

Al Capp poses with his lesson on saluting, 1943.

by Maurice Horn

Commentators agree that the 1940s constitute the period in which Al Capp's *Li'l Abner* hit its stride and assumed the classic form we remember today. In the previous decade, the strip had hewed close to the familiar lines of parodic adventure, albeit with telling forays into social criticism and satire, trends that became more and more pronounced as the 1930s wore on. This emergence in a few short years from a hillbilly strip into the status of a major literary feature was paralleled by *Li'l Abner's* growing popular success (one of the few instances in comic strip history when popular and literary tastes conjoined). This was evidenced by the number of comic book reprints of the strip beginning in 1939, as well the 1940 adaptation of *Li'l Abner* to the movie screen. Therefore, as this volume unfolds, Capp could be expected to perform at the top of his imaginative and narrative powers—and he does.

The daily strip that opens this volume carries a highly symbolic date—December 9, 1941, two days after the bombing of Pearl Harbor and one day after the U.S. declaration of war on Japan. Two days after that, on December 11, Germany would declare war on the United States, which would reciprocate within 24 hours. As it turns out, this run of *Li'l Abner* almost exactly covers America's first full year of wartime, from its entry into the lists to the North African landings and the Battle of Stalingrad; from the clash at Midway Island to the struggle for Guadalcanal.

Since newspaper strips are delivered to the syndicates weeks in advance of actual publication dates, one can't expect to find an echo of the momentous happenings that were splattered all over the front and inside pages of newspapers at that time, but it is an indication of Capp's interest in topical matters (and his life-long love of the movies) that the first Abner adventure in this volume is an affectionate take-off on *Citizen Kane*.

There is poetic justice in the fact, since *Citizen Kane's* relative failure at the box office, coming as it did after a meteoric start, is blamed by

Maurice Horn is editor of The World Encyclopedia of Comics.

WAL-FRY MAH HIDE!!- THET SHAPE COULD NOT BELONG TO NO ONE ELSE BUT DANGEROUS DAN McPEW, TH' PROUDEST FIGHTIN' MAN IN ALL TH' HILLS!!

H-HYAR COME ONE OF 'EM!!!

DANGEROUS DAN McPEW-- YO' IS TH' MOST FEAR-LESS FIGHTIN' MAN IN ALL TH' HILLS-AN' HYAR YO' IS A-HIDIN' FUM A LOOTENUNT IN A GARBAGE CAN!!- IS YO' SKEERED?

IT HAIN'T THET AH'M SKEERED, LI'L ABNER-IT'S JEST THET AH'M PROUD AS ANY FOOL KIN PLAINLY SEE!!!

AH SEES!!

AH IS TOO DAWGONE PROUD TO SALUTE, THASS WHUT!!-AH HAIN'T GONNA KOW-TOW T' NOBODY!!!

SALUTIN' HAIN'T KOW-TOWIN', DANGEROUS DAN-FO' INSTANCE-WHEN YO' SALUTES A OFFICER, WHUT DO HE DO?

HE SALUTES ME BACK, NATCHERLY!

-SO YO' HAIN'T KOW-TOWIN' T' HIM ANY MORE THAN HE IS T' YO'!!!-A SALUTE IS MERELY TH' COURTEYUSS RE-COG-NISHUN BETWIXT TWO MEMBERS O' TH' ARMED FORCES. IN FACK, SALUTIN' IS A PRIVILIGE!!

A PRIVILIGE? HOW DOES YO' FIGGER THET OUT?

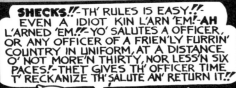

SHECKS!!-TH' RULES IS EASY!!- EVEN A IDIOT KIN L'ARN 'EM!-AH L'ARNED 'EM!!-YO' SALUTES A OFFICER, OR ANY OFFICER OF A FRIEN'LY FURRIN' COUNTRY IN UNIFORM, AT A DISTANCE O' NOT MORE'N THIRTY, NOR LESS'N SIX PACES!-THET GIVES TH' OFFICER TIME T' RECKANIZE TH' SALUTE AN' RETURN IT!!

-AN' WHEN YO' DOES SALUTE-BE SMART AN' SNAPPY 'BOUT IT!!-LOOK TH' OFFICER STRAIGHT IN TH' EYE - A CARELESS SALUTE, OR A SLOPPY OR HALF-HEARTED ONE IS DISCOURTEYUSS AN' DISRESPECTFUL!!'-IF TH' OFFICER REMAINS IN YO' VICINITY WIFOUT SPEAKIN' T' YO'-NO FURTHER SALUTE IS NECESSARY. IF A CONVERSAYSHUN TAKES PLACE BETWIXT TH' TWO O' YO', YO' SHOULD AGAIN SALUTE WHEN HE LEAVES!!!

NOW, EF THAR'S A GROUP O' SOLJERS, NOT IN FORMAY-SHUN, CALL TH' GROUP TO ATTENSHUN SOON AS YO' RECKANIZES AN' OFFICER APPROACHIN'. EF YO' IS ALL OUTA DOORS, EVERYONE SALUTES. EF INDOORS, OR IN A TENT, YO' SIMPLY REMOVES YO' HEAD-COVERIN' AN' STAND AT ATTENTION, UNLESS OTHERWISE DIRECTED!

THAR'S A FEW MORE SIMPLE RULES LIKE, FO' INSTANCE, YO' DON'T HAFTA SALUTE WHEN BOTH ARMS IS BEIN' USED T' CARRY OR HOLD SOME-THIN'. THEY IS ALL IN TH' SOLJER'S HAN'BOOK, RIGHT HYAR!!

Li'l Abner . . . By Al Capp.

most film critics on the outbreak of hostilities, along with William Randolph Hearst's unholy wrath. Abner's search for "Cherry Blossom" is a clear reference to the search for Kane's "Rosebud" in the movie, and it comes as a further wink on Capp's part that Abner's secret, like Kane's, is buried deep within the folds of childhood memories. As though these clues weren't enough, the artist further tips his hand by having Orson Welles himself appear in a featured part, as Orville Wolf, the latest in a long list of would-be Daisy Mae seducers. Perhaps Capp was repaying a debt to *Citizen Kane's* studio, RKO, which had also produced the *Li'l Abner* movie the preceding year; more likely he was repaying a debt to Welles who, on a previous occasion, had said a few kind words about Capp's creation. However that may be, the sequence shows how closely attuned to its times *Li'l Abner* could be.

As 1942 inexorably unfolds (and after that, all the other agonizingly slow years of wartime) the reader might be forgiven for expecting to see the *Abner* strip reflect the vicissitudes, agonies and triumphs of the war—especially at a time when most newspaper strips, like Milton Caniff's *Terry and the Pirates*, were rushing headlong into the fray. There are a few echoes of the struggle to be found in the Sunday page, particularly in the *Abner* topper, *Advice fo' Chillun*. Even in the daily strips reprinted here there are a few hints now and then. "Support the USO" stamps can be found with increasing frequency plastered on walls and car doors, and allusions to contemporary events are occasionally mouthed by one character or another. Joe Btfsplk, the world's worst jinx, announces in his very first daily appearance: "Home agin! Wal—ah spent a very injoyable winter wif Hitler in Russia!" In the strip for Christmas Day, Mammy untypically extends the love of her boy to all other boys: "In other words, we gotta treat 'em like we want other folks t'treat *our* boys!! *All* of 'em is *somebody's* boys—all of 'em is fine boys!!"

Yet, compared to the sentiments expressed in other newspaper strips of the period, this is paltry stuff. It is as though Capp didn't want to look down all the dark implications of the war in his comic strip. It is therefore legitimate to ask the question: why?

In her introduction to Volume 5 of this series, Julie Capp Cairol explains that her father "wanted Dogpatch to be a kind of refuge both from and for the world—a reminder of peace." And indeed, the July 4, 1942, strip makes this explicit. Al Capp was a complex individual, however, and there must have been more complex reasons for his deliberate avoidance in *Li'l Abner* of the central event of the 20th century: World War II. That he couldn't let Li'l Abner enlist in the Army, as so many other comic strip heroes were busily doing, seems natural enough. Abner in uniform would have been a greater comfort to the Axis than to the Allies. There also must have been the realization that, next to the Gestapo and the SS, Black Rufe and the murderous Scraggs were pikers, and that, compared to the Thousand Year Reich and German-occupied Europe, Dogpatch was a positive Eden. History, in all its hideousness, was striking at the very rationale of the *Abner* universe; yet Capp was artist enough to be able to transcend the strip's premises. He chose not to do so, however.

It is quite possible that the contrary-minded Capp didn't want to be seen following the mob of cartoonists who had jumped with both feet on the opportunity the war gave them for refreshing their tired plots or adopting a new outlook. Capp was no camp follower, and he might have been afraid that, had he joined the crowd, *Li'l Abner* would have become just another propagandizing, morale-boosting strip. In addition, the exigencies of war are restricting for the true creator: patriotism and natural empathy would no doubt have severely curtailed the strip's outrageous satire; and Capp must have been alert to the dangers that too great an identification with his characters would further undermine the strip's esthetic purposes.

There is also the matter of Ham Fisher and *Joe Palooka*. During his years of penuriousness, Capp had spent some time ghosting the strip for Fisher, and it is there that he claimed to have created the hillbilly characters of Big Leviticus and his cohorts. Fisher vehemently denied the claim. In the years intervening, Capp and Fisher had gone their separate and successful ways. Fisher had been one of the very first cartoonists to support the administration's war-preparedness program. In 1940, he had Palooka enlist in the Army and follow the stages of basic training, all of which were depicted in tones of unbridled enthusiasm, with the result that both Palooka and Fisher had been commended by President Roosevelt and Secretary for War Henry Stimson. Capp must

have been understandably reluctant to take on this superpatriotic friend of presidents and war secretaries on his own ground. As late as 1942, he found it within himself to praise his erstwhile employer in the piece he contributed to Martin Sheridan's *Comics and Their Creators*: "I worked with Fisher for several months and owe most of my success to him, for I learned many tricks of the trade while working alongside of him." For his part, Fisher never neglected an opportunity to take pot-shots at his former employee. In the same Sheridan book he averred that "many comics are based on hillbillies since I first used Big Leviticus in my strip." To top it off, in 1942 Fisher brought Leviticus back into *Joe Palooka* to have him take part in the North African campaign. Capp may have decided *not* to send his hillbillies into battle so as to avoid any unwelcome comparisons.

The brutalizing effects of the war couldn't be ignored, however, and their impact on Capp and his strip can be discerned in oblique but reveal-ing ways. A mounting savagery courses through many of the wartime adventures, starting with the episode in this volume in which the Scraggs are hired by the physically and morally repulsive J. P. Fangsby, "America's number one sportsman hog-breeder," to kidnap the Yokums' pet pig Salomey as a mate for his prize porker, Boar Scarloff. In carry-ing out their assignment, the Scraggs display a callousness and wanton disregard for human life that is unprecedented, even for them. At one point, after they have nabbed the hapless Gus Goosegrease by mistake, they kick him over a precipice, and to Fangsby's horrified protestations Romeo Scragg replies: "So what? Yo' said he were absolutely wor-thless." After having finally captured Salomey and received their thou-sand dollar reward, the same Romeo modestly acknowledges Fangsby's congratulations in these words: "Shecks! 'Twarn't nuthin'!! We didn't hafta kill more'n nine or ten folks!" The episode concludes with Fangsby being barbecued by the Scraggs—although by mistake—and served as the main dish at the banquet he had prepared for his fellow hog breeders.

Even more disturbing, because the villains of the piece are not caricatural Dogpatch outlaws, is the last episode to appear in this volume: to revive the sagging career of senile movie star Lorna Goon, her manager

---

At left, Abner promotes gas rationing, which began in 1942.

conspires to set up Li'l Abner in such a way that the youth would seem to have committed suicide for the love of the aging Lorna, by substituting real bullets for the blanks Abner thinks are in the gun.

In these and other *Abner* narratives, Capp can be seen veering sharp-ly away from satirical farce to black comedy. In this respect he is not far removed from film director Ernst Lubitsch, who was then traveling much the same road in such movies as *To Be Or Not to Be*. (It must be noted that Lubitsch chose to confront evil head-on by setting his com-edy smack in the middle of Nazi-occupied Warsaw.) If, as Alan Gowans has suggested in *The Unchanging Arts*, Al Capp's *Li'l Abner* "was a comment and allegory on the historic American dream and what was happening to it in the mid-20th century" (and this is the generally ac-cepted view of the strip), then at least every other story from the period 1942-45 is a comment and allegory (however oblique) on the war's impact on American society.

It would be wrong to assume that the war was Capp's only preoc-cupation at the time. He was then at the height of his creative powers and took advantage of his increasing creativity not only to spin topical allegories, but also to further elaborate the Dogpatch mythos and enlarge his already sizeable cast of characters. Some of the new faces of 1942 are, in addition to Joe Btfsplk, the aptly-named Barney Barnsmell and his even more malodorous cousin Big Barnsmell ("th' *inside* man at th' skonk works"), not forgetting such colorful bit players as a telegram-singing hillbilly, a psychoanalyst named Dr. Jekyll, a prizefighter called Battlin' Cherry Blossom, "Beer Barrel" Polkis the Polish sport, and an organ grinder and pet billed as "Adolfo and his monkey Benito" (ah, the war again). Numerous enough to field a small team are the variably-gifted scions of the Jones clan: the jack-of-all trades Available ("Ah is *allus* available to mah friends—fo' a *price*, natcherly!"), and his cousins Disgustin' ("Yo' *is* disgustin', Disgustin'!"), Embraceable (whose charms no male—except Li'l Abner—is able to resist), Unbearable (whose presence even Abner can't bear), and Unmentionable (whose aspect is so horrifying Capp only dares to show his hairy arms and legs).

In addition to his fanciful flights of topicality, Capp also had recourse to more conventional forms of humor, firmly setting himself in the American traditon of Mark Twain, Finley Peter Dunne ("Mr. Dooley"),

and even Will Rogers, at those not infrequent times when he turns sen-timental. Some examples will suffice. After Abner bumps heads with the bull known as "Black Death" and is laid out as dead, the Mexican attendants return and discover he's disappeared. "We laid the dad Americano out here—an' covered hees face weeth an Americano newspaper!! Now—both are gone," muses one. "Ah well—the Americano was of no use since he was dad—but that newspaper had Americano fonnies een eet!!", bewails the other. To Nosey McBlabber who unexpectedly shows up at his own murder trial to deny he has been killed despite the issuance of an official death certificate, the presiding judge indignantly retorts: "It says hyar, plain as day—Yo' is daid!! It got a official gov'munt stamp on it!! Ah hopes yo' won't try to insinooate th' gov'munt is a *liar!!*", and then goes on: "Dogpatch is a modern, intellygunt *un*sooperstishus commoonity—an' we don't believe in ghosts—so—*ah gives yo' ten minutes t'git outa this commoonity, ghost!!*"

And finally, a very American bit of self-deprecating humor. After having given up his fruitless search for Cherry Blossom, Abner resigns himself to the fate Dr. Jekyll had forecast for him in case of failure, with these words: "R-reckon ah better g-go back t'Dogpatch an' lose mah mind—(gulp)—thar's no *better* place t'lose it!!"

While 1942 is a pivotal year, questions about the road not taken still nag the mind. With the hounds of war unleashed all over the globe, why are only a few feeble yelps heard in *Li'l Abner*? Granted that Capp for multiple reasons couldn't send his protagonists to the front lines, he could have let the war come to them, as Chester Gould did with *Dick Tracy*. One can easily imagine how spies, saboteurs, fifth colum-nists, German-American bund members, and other "Axis rats" would have become fodder for Capp's savage wit and relentless satire. Capp's poison pen would have worked wonders on such live targets, and these would have provided sources of black humor in ways the fictional Scraggs could never achieve. Barring that, Capp could have used the war as a background, the way such strips as *Dixie Dugan* or *Freckles and His Friends* did, and comment on the issues by indirection.

Yet Capp chose to do none of these things. In spite of speculation, the mystery, like Sherlock Holmes' dog that didn't bark in the night, may never be solved.

1942: War Work

by Dave Schreiner

In late 1941, the United States entered the European and Asian war, making it worldwide. As stated in Maurice Horn's introduction, Al Capp did not directly invite the war into *Li'l Abner*. He devoted several strips in successive years to explain why. The first appeared on July 4, 1942, and it set the tone for those that showed up in 1943 and 1944.

Dear Friends:
This seems the right day to answer a question many of you have asked me — "When is Li'l Abner going into the Army?"
Li'l Abner isn't going into the Army. And this is why —
Perhaps Li'l Abner and his friends, living through these terrible days in a peaceful, happy, free world, will do their part — by thus reminding us that this is what we are fighting for — to have that world again. A world where a fella can do pretty much as he pleases as long as he doesn't bother his neighbors — a world where a fella can worship God in his own way — and where the next fella's got the same right — a world where a fella and his gal can look up at the moon just for the foolishness of it — and not because there may be planes up there coming to blast 'em both off the earth — a world where a fella is free to be as wise or foolish as he pleases — but, mainly, — an earth where a fella is free!!
That world has disappeared — until we win this war. Perhaps this small section of our daily newspaper can do its part best by helping us to remember that a free world once did exist — and will again!!

—Al Capp

So the war stayed out of *Li'l Abner*, although gas rationing, blackouts and other manifestations of homefront inconveniences showed up when Capp needed them for plot. Perhaps he felt that bringing the war into the strip trivialized what was going on across the oceans. It's quite possible that he felt contempt for those strips that were facilely patriotic; that jumped on the bandwagon for little other purpose than to stop questions about why a character wasn't in uniform. Perhaps he wanted to guard his characters from embarrassing fits of unrealistic flagwaving. Perhaps he knew that as the war went on, mindless morale-boosting patriotism would come face to face with reality, and would crumble into cynicism. Contrary to propaganda, the GIs actually fighting the war weren't fighting for apple pie and baseball, they were struggling to stay alive, and perhaps Capp felt that any easy patriotism on his part would in the long run make the strip look foolish.

And maybe he just couldn't see a good way to make room for the war in his increasingly satirical humorous plotline, and he sincerely wanted to make the strip a little oasis away from the content of the rest of the newspaper. Capp was not a booster in the *Li'l Abner* of 1941-2, he was becoming a commentator. However, he was extremely active in contributing his considerable artistic talents to the war effort outside the strip itself.

On this page, a Post Office poster promoting Savings Bonds. At left, opposite page, Capp's SMALL CHANGE was syndicated free to newspapers by the Treasury Department.

He saved his war work for special jobs, for the military, the Red Cross, and the War Bond Division of the Treasury Department. For the latter he created *Small Change*, initially called *Small Fry* until the more propitious title presented itself. It was the first strip ever syndicated by the U.S. government. A Sunday page, it concerned the efforts of the title character to promote enough pocket change to buy war bonds at $18.75 a pop. Rejected by the military as physically unfit, Small Change will do anything honest to make money for bonds, and he lectures various slackers he meets along the way to buy bonds, too. At least 75 of these pages exist. Capp was paid a dollar per year for the strip, which was the rate of wartime pay for certain high-powered consultants and executives who made their real money elsewhere. Capp later told E. J. Kahn, Jr., in a *New Yorker* profile, that he once tried to claim $8,000 expenses one year for producing the strip, and it was denied. The Internal Revenue Service allegedly told him that "a man with a dollar-a-year job ought to have better sense than to shell out eight thousand times that amount on incidental expenses."

For the military, he did a series of posters addressing such matters as saluting and venereal disease. The VD poster was rejected, as was one done by Milton Caniff. As Caniff told it later, "They turned down my poster because my bad girls were too good looking. They turned down Al's because he overplayed it a bit. They knew he had the audience and they were anxious to get him involved, but he couldn't quite find the handle they wanted. They wanted to be specific about condoms, but not *too* specific. They could get drawings done by somebody who wasn't well known, and that could illustrate the little book the chaplain or medic gave you. If they had a cartoonist like Al, the poster he did would almost defeat itself. The men would be looking at Li'l Abner and what he said about it, ha ha ha, instead of the message."

Capp told Kahn that he had problems with the VD strip well before it was rejected. The chaste, woman-fearing Abner was the star of these educational posters; they were all labeled "Private Li'l Abner."

"I couldn't very well point up the horrors of venereal diseases without having somebody catch one," Capp said. "But I was damned if I'd

Al Capp meets Veronica Lake, inspiration of "Cherry Blossom." The inscription reads: "To Al, creator of my greatest competitor, Cherry Blossom. May good luck always be yours. Sincerely, Veronica Lake." Lake's trademark "peekaboo" hairstyle was a prewar fashion hit. On page 12, SMALL CHANGE began life as SMALL FRY.

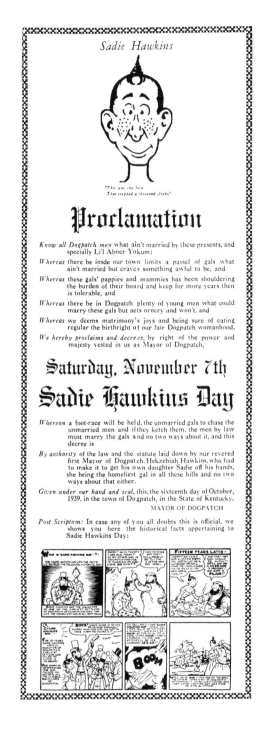

destroy the technical perfection of my boy even for my country." One of Abner's friends was elected, as also happened in the How to Salute poster reprinted elsewhere in this volume. The VD poster passed through some channels of the military unscathed, but was finally rejected by the Chief of Chaplains.

Late in the war, Capp wrote and drew *Al Capp by Li'l Abner*, a booklet for servicemen-amputees distributed by the Red Cross. In it, Abner, in his inimitable way, recounts how Capp lost his left leg in an accident at age nine, and how he adjusted to the trauma. From touring military hospitals and personal experience, Capp knew the biggest problem amputees faced was acceptance. They were depressed, they resented pity, and they feared their sex lives were over. His comic book addressed these feelings. He acknowledged the problems he had learning to use a prosthetic device. He admitted feeling self-conscious around even old friends after the accident. A major portion of the book dealt with Capp's courtship of Catherine Cameron and their marriage. The book had a sunny outlook, emphasizing a stiff-upper-lip approach appropriate to the context, and it didn't fully reflect the difficulties Capp had had in learning to walk with a wooden leg.

Elliott Caplin, Capp's younger brother, recalls that when Al volunteered to tour hospitals, doctors initially banned him from the wards. If the amputees thought they would walk as badly as Capp, the doctors said, "they'd blow their brains out." Capp had to learn from an expert how to walk correctly. It was so painful that after the war, he went back to his old way. The Caplin family had been too poor to afford the different legs young Al needed to keep pace with his growth. Instead of progressing through eight legs from the age of nine until he reached his full growth, Elliott estimates he had two. Extending an existing device to compensate for growth didn't work. Somehow, Capp fashioned his own way of walking, which apparently was utilitarian but not pretty. During his war tours, though, he painfully walked in a morale-boosting way.

• • •

The 1942 run of *Li'l Abner* introduced two characters that stand out in a stellar year of humor and tall tales. One was a long-nosed little hustler named Available Jones. His motto: "I can be had—for a price!" If he wasn't

so amiably dumb, and honest by his own standards, and didn't have such an endless family, Available could pass for Sammy Glick in *What Makes Sammy Run?* However, Capp didn't view Available in the same indignant light author Budd Schulberg viewed Sammy. It's obvious that Capp liked Available, as was right, since the character was so instantly...available...for any sort of plot twist. Every variety of human (and inhuman) animal funneled through Available's office in the years following 1942, and all of them somehow brought misery to Abner. Available started a lot of stories that Abner had to finish.

The other character was Joe Btfsplk, world's worst jinx. He became one of Capp's most famous creations, even if nobody could pronounce his name. For starting, and then twisting, and then rescuing plots, Joe and Available were hard to beat.

• • •

While Capp was having a banner year with his strip, construction of a huge military complex began on 59,000 acres in an isolated and primitive area along the Clinch River in eastern Tennessee. The top secret complex was in the Appalachian foothills and it was being built to isolate and enrich a radioactive isotope to be used in a new and powerful weapon under intense planning near Los Alamos, New Mexico. The fenced reservation was called the Clinton Engineer Works. The rough town being built within the fence was named Oak Ridge. The workers and the residents, who were to live within the fence for the next two years, called the whole mess "Dogpatch."

At left, newspapers let their readers know when Sadie Hawkins Day occurred in 1942.

Caniff, Milton, "The Two Minute Furlough," *The Complete Male Call*, Kitchen Sink Press, Princeton, Wis., 1985.

Caplin, Elliott, "We Called Him Alfred...," *Cartoonist ProFiles*, 1979

Fussell, Paul, *Wartime: Understanding and Behavior in the Second World War*, Oxford University Press, New York, 1989.

Grun, Bernard, *The Timetables of History: A Horizontal Linkage of People and Events*, Simon & Schuster, New York, 1975.

Kahn, E. J., Jr. "OOFF!!! (SOB!!) EEP!!! (GULP!!) ZOWIE!!!!—II, *The New Yorker*, 1947.

Manchester, William, *The Glory and the Dream, A Narrative History of America, 1932-1972*, Little, Brown and Co., Boston, 1973.

Rhodes, Richard, *The Making of the Atomic Bomb*, Simon & Schuster, New York, 1986.

The Two Lorna Goons

On November 25, 1942, the aging Hollywood actress Lorna Goon made her debut in *Li'l Abner*. Vain, arrogant, ghoulish in appearance, the name was a perfect fit.

Trouble is, in September of 1941, another Lorna Goon had appeared, this one the plain-Jane fiance of Barney Barnsmell, pictured at left.

Granted, the first Lorna was a bit player, and would not appear again, and the name was too good for Al Capp not to reuse.

But Lorna Goon appeared a second time because of an emergency. The second Lorna was originally named Scarlett O'Horror, as any fool who looks at the panel on the right can plainly see. In October of 1942, Capp had begun his aborted parody of Margaret Mitchell's *Gone With the Wind* on the Sunday page [see volume five's introductory material]. The first page in the projected four-Sunday strip sequence met with an immediate negative reaction from Mitchell and her lawyer husband. They started a suit charging copyright infringement, and Capp and United Features Syndicate were forced to apologize in a Sunday page of December, 1942.

Before the storm from Atlanta broke over his head, Capp had begun producing the daily strip featuring Scarlett O'Horror. He was forced to go back and hastily paste over the offending name and reletter it Lorna Goon before it was published.

Judging from the space left over in balloons, the pasteovers continued for a number of weeks. While all this mechanical work was a nuisance, Capp's narrative did not suffer, and he covered the change most admirably in the strip of December 16, when Abner sends his love poem to the actress. It is obvious the last two lines of the poem originally read:

> *Ah'd druther jump in the lake tomorrow*
> *Than not get no letter from Scarlett O'Horror.*

He revised it to:

> *Ah'd druther jump in the lake tomorrow noon*
> *Than not get no letter from Lorna Goon.*

The revision doesn't quite scan, but then Abner doesn't quite scan, either.

—D.S.

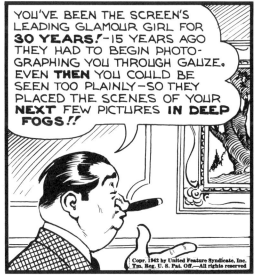

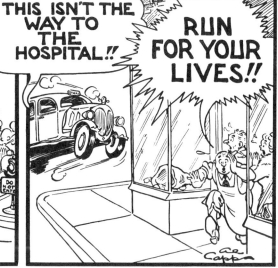

LI'L ABNER

by AL CAPP!!

LI'L ABNER by AL CAPP!!

20

Li'l ABNER *by* AL CAPP!!

LI'L ABNER by AL CAPP !!

LI'L ABNER

by **AL CAPP!!**

LI'L ABNER

by AL CAPP!!

(="THIS IS TH' **FOURTH** BATHIN' SUIT SHE'S PUT ON —BUT—GULP!—AH **STILL** CAIN'T SEE HER EARS!") N-NO, MA'M, AH CAIN'T TELL EF YO' IS TH' TYPE IN **THET** SUIT, EITHER!

I'LL TRY ANOTHER!

12-30

(="**STILL** CAIN'T SEE HER EARS!") N-NO, MA'M! — **THET** WON'T DO, EITHER!!

YOU FRESH THING!! — I DON'T BELIEVE YOU **ARE** A TALENT SCOUT!!

OUCH!! — YO' IS POW'FUL RIGHT MA'M — AH IS MERELY A BOY, LOOKIN' FO' CHERRY BLOSSOM WIF TH' HEART-SHAPED EARS — SOB!!

226

AH SEEN HER EARS WHEN SHE BASHED ME. **WRONG SHAPE!!**

TH' SEARCH GOES ON!!

Copr. 1941 by United Feature Syndicate, Inc.
Tm. Reg. U.S. Pat. Off.—All rights reserved

A-PININ' FO' LI'L ABNER HAIN'T GONNA MAKE YO' A **BRIDE!** EF YO' CAIN'T NAB **HIM** — SET YO' CAP FO' **SOMEBODY ELSE!!**

DON'T WANT SOMEBODY ELSE! ONLY **HIM!**

LETTER FUM SOMEBODY! KINELY READ IT, DAISY MAE.

12-31
777

Dear Sister Pansy:
Li'l Abner will not be coming home for a long, long time!

He is suffering from an obscure psychological complex revolving about his frustrated love for an actual although elusive female individual to whom he refers in only the most enigmatic terms.

As a result of exhaustive psychoanalysis the expert opinion is that he must locate this girl and then, let us hope, his subconscious affection for her will result in a happy marriage.
affectionately,
Bessie

THEM IS **MIGHTY** PURTY WORDS — BUT WHUT DO IT **MEAN**?

ALL AH GIT OUTA IT IS THET—H-HE IS IN LOVE OF A SARTIN GAL — AN' WHEN HE FINDS HER, HE OUGHTA M-MARRY UP WIF HER!!

NOW WILL YO' STOP A-WASTIN' YO' TIME, AN' GIT OUT AN' TRAP YO'SELF A **HUSBIN!**

Copr. 1941 by United Feature Syndicate, Inc.
Tm. Reg. U.S. Pat. Off.—All rights reserved

Li'L ABNER by AL CAPP !!

Li'l ABNER

by AL CAPP!!

28

LI'L ABNER

by AL CAPP !!

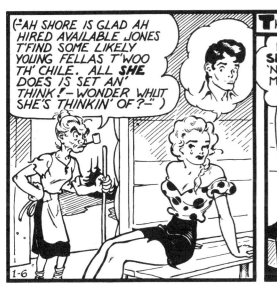

("AH SHORE IS GLAD AH HIRED AVAILABLE JONES T'FIND SOME LIKELY YOUNG FELLAS T'WOO TH' CHILE. ALL **SHE** DOES IS SET AN' THINK!—WONDER WHUT SHE'S THINKIN' OF?—")

THE OFFICES OF AVAILABLE JONES.

HM!—NARY A **SINGLE** BOY GOOD 'NUFF FO' DAISY MAE, ON MAH LIST---

BABIES MINDED

DRY BABIES 5¢

OTHER BABI 10¢ AND UP

ARE YOU AVAILABLE JONES?

IF IT'S TOO UNPLEASANT TO DO IT—I'LL DO IT—FOR A PRICE!

1-6

—AH HAS TH' HONOR AN' PRIVILEGE O' BEIN' HIM!

I'VE HEARD ABOUT YOU. YOU RUN A SORT OF **DATE BUREAU**, DON'T YOU?

NOT A **DATE** BUREAU, SUH! A **MARRIAGE** BUREAU!—AH DON'T HAVE NO TRUCK WIF NO FELLAS UNLESS THEY GOT **MATRIMONIAL INTENSHUNS!**—HAS **YO'** GOT MATRIMONIAL INTENSHUNS?

OH, SURE!—I'VE GOT **ALL** KINDS OF INTENTIONS. I'M LOOKING FOR A CUTE LITTLE NUMBER. I'M ORVILLE WOLF—OF NEW YORK.—

Copr. 1942 by United Feature Syndicate, Inc.
Tm. Reg. U. S. Pat. Off.—All rights reserved

782

I'M A TERRIBLY LONESOME KID! ARE THERE ANY CUTE LITTLE NUMBERS AVAILABLE, AVAILABLE?

EF AH **DOES** INTRODUCE YO' TO A SUITABLE YOUNG LADY IS YO' WILLIN' T'MARRY HER, SETTLE DOWN, AN' RAISE A FAMBLY?

OH, **SURE!!**— (—THIS SURVEYING JOB ENDS IN TWO WEEKS—JUST TIME FOR A QUICK ROMANCE—AND THEN I LEAVE FOR MY NEXT JOB—IN ALASKA—**ALONE!**—)

HM—YO' HAS STEADY WORK—THASS FINE!—IS YO' IN GOOD HEALTH?

ARE YOU LOOKING FOR A MATE? I WILL FIND ONE FOR YOU DESIRABLE ONES 1.00 UNDESIRABLES—.10¢

1-7

I'M IN THE PINK EXCEPT FOR **ONE MINOR FLAW!**—I HAVE A **SUPER-SENSITIVE NASAL PASSAGE!**—FOR INSTANCE, I CAN TELL THERE'S A SMALL BRUSH FIRE ABOUT A **MILE** FROM HERE AND THAT THE MAN WHO IS TRYING TO STOMP IT OUT HASN'T CHANGED HIS SOCKS IN TWO WEEKS!

YO' IS WONDIFUL!

AVAILABLE JONES

Copr. 1942 by United Feature Syndicate, Inc.
Tm. Reg. U. S. Pat. Off.—All rights reserved

783

AH HAPPENS T'KNOW THAT IS **EXACKLY WHUT'S HAPPENIN'**. FANTASTIC BROWN **IS** TRYIN' T'STOMP OUT A SMALL BRUSH FIRE— AN' IT **HAS** BIN ONLY TWO WEEKS SINCE HE PUT ON HIS WINTER SOCKS!

YAWN! HOW ABOUT THOSE CUTE NUMBERS?

LI'L ABNER

by AL CAPP!!

SEAL OF APPROVAL

THIS CARD INDICATES THAT *Orville Wolf* -- HAS PAID HIS FEE IN ADVANCE AND IS ENTITLED TO WOO *Daisy Mae Scragg.*

SIGNED *Available Jones*

WELL, I CONVINCED JONES THAT I'M A FINE, UPRIGHT CHAP—HE SAID THIS DAISY MAE IS A BEAUTY—BUT, IF SHE LOOKS ANYTHING LIKE **SOME** OF THE BEAUTIES I'VE SEEN AROUND HERE—I'LL SPEND MOST OF MY EVENINGS PLAYING **SOLITAIRE!**

Copr. 1942 by United Feature Syndicate, Inc.
Tm. Reg. U.S. Pat. Off.—All rights reserved   1-8

HM!—YO' GOT TH' AVAILABLE JONES SEAL OF APPROVAL, SO AH RECKON YO' IS SATISFACT'RY! HAS YO' GOT STEADY WORK?

YES, MA'M.

THEN—YO' KIN START A-WOOIN' MAH GRAN' CHILE, NAME OF DAISY MAE!

H-HOWDY, STRANGER.

HOWDY! (—SHE'S **GORGEOUS**—AND **DUMB!** JUST **MY** TYPE!—)

WOULD YOU PERMIT ME TO TAKE DAISY MAE OUT FOR A LITTLE RIDE IN THE MOONLIGHT?

SHO' NUFF, STRANGER!—YO' GOT TH' AVAILABLE JONES SEAL OF APPROVAL, AN' THASS GOOD-NUFF FO' **ME!**

(—"SHE'S BEAUTIFUL AND DUMB!—JUST THE TYPE THAT **USUALLY** FALLS FOR MY HIGH-PRESSURE LINE! AND IT'S EASY TO SEE SHE'S **THRILLED** TO BE WITH ME!"—)

(—"A BALMY NIGHT—AN' A LOVELY YALLER MOON!—OH, IT'D BE SO THRILLIN' EF AH WERE WIF TH' **RIGHT** BOY—BUT, AH **HAINT!**"—)

1-9

BUT—?—?—IT WERE **SO** NICE A-RIDIN'—AN' BESIDES, AH HAS LOOKED AT TH' MOON FUM THIS RIVER BANK **MANY** TIMES BEFO'!

THAT OLD MOON IS GOING TO LOOK A LOT **DIFFERENT** TO YOU TONIGHT, DAISY MAE!!

Copr. 1942 by United Feature Syndicate, Inc.
Tm. Reg. U.S. Pat. Off.—All rights reserved

AT THAT MOMENT—PHILADELPHIA!

NO MO' CHERRY BLOSSOMS IN NOO YAWK—SO AH CONTINUES TH' SEARCH HYAR!!

OH, CHERRY BLOSSOM! **WHAR** IS YO'? **WHO** IS YO'?

SOB!!

LI'L ABNER by AL CAPP!!

LI'L ABNER
by AL CAPP!!

GOODNIGHT, DAISY MAE. I'LL BE SEEING YOU TOMORROW NIGHT —AT THE USUAL TIME—

(SIGH!) AH S'POSE SO, MISTAH WOLF!—

1-13

FOR FIVE CONSECUTIVE NIGHTS—I'VE TAKEN HER OUT AND HANDED HER EVERY LINE IN MY REPERTOIRE.—I'VE USED EVERY APPROACH —AND I CAN'T GET TO FIRST BASE!!

SHE DOESN'T SEEM TO EVEN KNOW I'M WITH HER —OR CARE!—HER THOUGHTS SEEM A THOUSAND MILES AWAY. —SIGH!—IT'S A HARD FIGHT—BUT A WOLF NEVER GIVES UP!—AT LEAST I HAVE NO COMPETITION!!

AT THAT MOMENT—COMING 'ROUND THE MOUNTAIN.

WE OUGHTA REACH AVAILABLE JONES'S BY MORNIN'—

(SNIFF!—SNIFF!) MUST BE A TANNERY BURNIN' SOMEWHAR. AH'LL CLOSE ALL TH' WINDOWS!—

WHY REMAIN SINGLE? I WILL INTRODUCE YOU TO A GIRL FAT GIRLS—50¢ BOW-LAIGED GIRLS—10¢

ARE YOU MAD AT THE WORLD? KICK ME IN THE TEETH FOR A NICKEL

1-14

AH CLOSED ALL TH' WINDOWS—BUT (SNIFF) IT'S AS POWERFUL AS EVAH!—IT'S SOMETHIN' IN THIS ROOM—AN' IT HAINT HOOMIN!!

NATCHERLY! IT'S ME!!

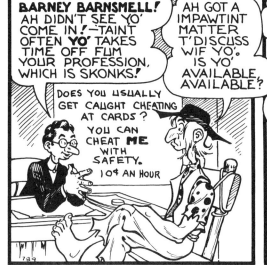

BARNEY BARNSMELL! AH DIDN'T SEE YO' COME IN!—TAINT OFTEN YO' TAKES TIME OFF FUM YOUR PROFESSION, WHICH IS SKONKS!

AH GOT A IMPAWTINT MATTER T'DISCUSS WIF YO'. IS YO' AVAILABLE, AVAILABLE?

DOES YOU USUALLY GET CAUGHT CHEATING AT CARDS? YOU CAN CHEAT ME WITH SAFETY. 10¢ AN HOUR

YES-BUT (SNIFF!)—AH STILL GITS IT—IT HAINT YO'—IT'S SOMETHIN' EVEN WORSE!

MUST BE MAH COUSIN BIG BARNSMELL—HE'S TH' INSIDE MAN AT TH' SKONK WORKS!

WAL-TELL HIM T'GO AWAY FUM TH' DOOR!!

HE HAINT AT TH' DOOR. HE'S AT TH' CREEK—TWO MILES AWAY—

Li'l ABNER by AL CAPP!!

SO IT'S (*SNIFF! SNIFF!*)-YO' COUSIN, BIG BARNSMELL AH (*CHOKE!*) NOTICES-AN' HE'S TWO MILES AWAY **MY!!**-

YO' SEE, HE'S TH' **INSIDE** MAN AT TH' SKONK WORKS. SO, NATCHERLY, YO' KIN TELL HE'S AROUND, WHEN TH' WIND IS UP!

MAH COUSIN IS A FINE, HARD-WORKIN' YOUNG FELLA, AN' **VERY ROMANTICAL**-BUT HE FINDS IT HARD T'GIT ACQUAINTED WIF GALS.

NATCHERLY!

HE WOULD LIKE T'GIT MARRIED UP! HAS YO' ANY SUITABLE YOUNG LADIES AVAILABLE, AVAILABLE?

YES-AH GOT **ONE**-BUT AH'D HAFTA LOOK TH' APPLICANT OVER BEFO' AH C'D GIVE HIM MAH SEAL OF APPROVAL-

THASS **EASY!! COME HYAR, COUSIN!** -HE'S **A-COMIN'!**

(*CHOKE!-*) Y-YES-AH NOTICES HE IS-ON S-SECOND THOUGHT, MEBBE HE'D BETTER GO TEN MILES AWAY, T'PINEAPPLE JUNCTION-HAVE HIS **PITCHER** TAKEN-AN' **SEND IT T'ME!!**-

1-15

AH FINALLY GOT YO' TH' SEAL OF APPROVAL, COUSIN. THET ENTITLES YO' T'WOO DAISY MAE WIF MATREE-MONIAL INTENSHUNS!-AN' NOW-AH'D LIKE T'LEAVE YO'!

NATCHERLY!

(*-I'VE TRIED THE SAME HIGH-PRESSURE METHODS ON DAISY MAE THAT HAVE ALWAYS BEEN SO SUCCESSFUL WITH OTHER GIRLS-BUT SHE DOESN'T EVEN GIVE ME A NOD!-I WONDER-IF THERE'S SOMEONE ELSE -ON HER MIND-"*)

HAIN'T YO' TH' NEW SURVEYOR WHICH HAS BIN A-WOOIN' DAISY MAE?

HAW! IT'S **SO** AMOOZIN' T'WATCH YO' WOO HER WHEN ALL TH' TIME SHE **REALLY** LOVES LI'L ABNER. **HE'S GONE!**

(*'SO!-THERE IS SOMEONE ELSE!'*) THIS LI'L ABNER-HE MUST'VE BEEN A TERRIFIC WOOER TO HAVE WON DAISY MAE'S HEART!

SHECKS, NO! LI'L ABNER NEVAH WOOED DAISY MAE!-HE JEST TREATED HER **MIZZUBLE.** AN' (*CHUCKLE*) TH' MIZZUBLER HE TREATED HER-TH' MORE SHE LOVED HIM!

(*-SO!-THAT'S THE METHOD THAT GETS HER-THE ONE METHOD I HAVENT TRIED!-*)

1-16

LI'L ABNER by AL CAPP!!

("CHUCKLE!—WITHOUT REALIZING IT, PAPPY YOKUM TIPPED ME OFF ON THE **SURE-FIRE APPROACH** TO DAISY MAE!—HE TOLD ME **EXACTLY** HOW LI'L ABNER TREATED HER. APPARENTLY SHE RESPONDS TO **COMPLETE INDIFFERENCE**.")

("SIGH!—HYAR COME MISTAH WOLF **AGIN**!—AH WISHT HE'D LET ME ALONE, BUT HE'S **SO SWEET** AN' **COMPLIMENT'RY**, AN' **GENNULMANLY** T'ME—AH CAIN'T REFOOZE T'GO OUT WIF HIM!—

1-17

WELL—HERE I AM AGAIN TO TAKE YOU OUT BUT I'D RATHER GO FISHING—

YO' **WOULD**

ALONE!

?

?

NATURALLY!—IT'S A SHAME TO WASTE SUCH A BEAUTIFUL EVENING WITH A GIRL WHEN I COULD **ENJOY** IT WITH SOME CATFISH!

("SUDDENLY! —THAR IS SOMETHIN' ABOUT HIM—**THET FASCINATES ME!!**"—)

Copr. 1942 by United Feature Syndicate, Inc.
Tm. Reg. U. S. Pat. Off.—All rights reserved

792

IT WORKS!!

("AT LAST I HAVE THE KEY TO HER HEART—**INDIFFERENCE!** THE SAME TECHNIQUE LI'L ABNER USED!"—)

Y-YO'D REALLY RUTHER GO **FISHIN'**— THAN BE WIF **ME**?

NATURALLY!— **I'M** NO FOOL!— HUNTING AND FISHING ARE FUN—BUT **GIRLS**—HMPH!! ALL **GIRLS** WANT TO DO IS SNUGGLE UP AND **KISS**!!—

GULP!— D-DO YO' MIND EF AH SETS A LI'L CLOSER T'YO', LI'L AB-??—ER- AH MEANS, MISTAH WOLF!

1-19

793

I'M GOING TO PARK BY THIS RIVER —AND YEARN—

FO' **ME**?—

NAW!—FOR THE **CAT FISH** IN IT!!

WHILE ON THE OTHER SIDE OF THE RIVER THE HEART OF BIG BARNSMELL BREAKS!!—

AH GOT TH' SEAL OF APPROVAL—BUT AH HAIN'T GOT TH' NERVE T'**USE** IT!!

Copr. 1942 by United Feature Syndicate, Inc.
Tm. Reg. U. S. Pat. Off.—All rights reserved

LI'L ABNER
by AL CAPP!!

LI'L ABNER

by AL CAPP!!

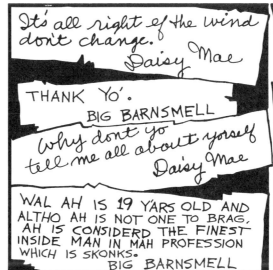

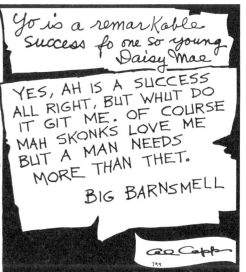

LI'L ABNER

by AL CAPP!!

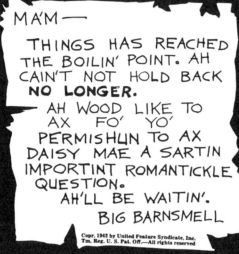

LI'L ABNER by AL CAPP!!

Dere Mister Barnsmell:
Yo proposal reserved. Mah granny says ah gotta marry somebody so it mite as well be yo.

But first ah wood like to go on a little trip alone.

Do not worry. ah will come back in a month and become yo bride.

respeckfully yorn
Miss Daisy Mae
Scragg.

YIPPAY!!— OH!!—AH'LL SPEND THIS MONTH WORKIN' AS AH HAS **NEVAH** WORKED BEFO'!—AH IS **INSPIRED**!!—AH WILL RISE T' TH' **TOP** O' MAH PROFESSION, WHICH IS **SKONKS**!!

EEP!! EEP!!

1-29
Copr. 1942 by United Feature Syndicate, Inc.
Tm. Reg. U. S. Pat. Off.—All rights reserved

PLEASE, GRANNY—DON'T AX ME **WHAR** AH'M GOIN'—OR **WHY**!—AH'LL BE BACK IN A MONTH AN' GO THROUGH WIF TH' MARRIAGE—

AN' THEN YO'LL BE A BARNSMELL!—AH, ME—MEBBE SOME DAY THIS LONELY HOUSE WILL BE FULL O' LI'L BARNSMELLS!

AND SO, THE BRIDE-TO-BE TRUDGES HER LONELY WAY—OUT OF THE HILLS—

LI'L ABNER'S SEARCH FOR "CHERRY BLOSSOM WITH THE HEART-SHAPED EARS" HAS LED SOUTH OF THE BORDER.

GULP!—AH'VE SEARCHED ALL THROUGH TH' YEW-NITED STATES—AN' CANADA—AN' NOW—HYAR——AN'—**AH CAIN'T FIND HER**!!

ENTRANCE
PLAZA DE TORO

1-30

TH' DOCTOR SAID EF AH **DIDN'T** FIND HER—AH'D LOSE MAH **MIND**!—THET MEANS AH WOULDN'T BE INTELLY-JUNT NO MO'!—AH COULDN'T STAND THET!—'DRUTHER BE DAID!—?!?!

NO!!— NO!!— I REFUSE! EET EES CERTAIN DEATH!!

Copr. 1942 by United Feature Syndicate, Inc.
Tm. Reg. U. S. Pat. Off.—All rights reserved

BUT—YOU ARE TH' G-R-REATEST BOOL-FIGHTER EEN ALL THE WORLD!!—EEF YOU REFUSE TO FIGHT "BLACK DEATH" YOU WILL LIVE IN DEESGRACE!!

AH, YES **BUT**—I WEEL—**LIVE**!!—TO FIGHT THAT BOOL EES **SUICIDE**!—ADIOS, CUCARACHAS!!

BUT—THE CROWD EES WAITING TO BE AMUSED!!

AH'LL FIGHT "BLACK DEATH"! EF AH **GOTTA** GO, AH MIGHT AS WELL GO IN A WAY THET'LL AMOOZE TH' CROWD!!

40

LI'L ABNER

by AL CAPP!!

SENSATIONAL NEW HOLLYWOOD DISCOVERY !!!

GLAMOURMOUNT PRODUCTIONS IS MAINTAINING A DEEP SECRECY ABOUT MISS CHERRY BLOSSOM, THEIR NEW STAR DISCOVERY, WHO HAS **TWICE** AS MUCH APPEAL AS VERONICA LAKE BECAUSE **HER** HAIR COVERS **BOTH** HER EYES!

ALL THAT THE PUBLIC KNOWS ABOUT HER IS THAT SHE SUDDENLY APPEARED IN HOLLYWOOD A WEEK AGO, AND SPEAKS WITH A SOFT SOUTHERN ACCENT.

THE STUDIO IS KEEPING HER IN ABSOLUTE SECLUSION. NO VISITORS ARE ALLOWED TO SEE HER OR SPEAK WITH HER.

MISS CHERRY BLOSSOM

2-3

?-?-WE LAID THE DAD AMERICANO OUT **HERE** - AN' COVERED HEES FACE WEETH AN **AMERICANO NEWSPAPER!!** - NOW - **BOTH** ARE **GONE!!**

AH, WELL-THE AMERICANO WAS OF NO USE SINCE HE WAS DAD - BUT THAT NEWSPAPER HAD **AMERICANO FONNIES EEN EET!!**

SIGH!! - NOW WE WEEL **NEVAIRE** KNOW EEF SENOR ABNAIRE WEEL MARRY UP WEETH SENORITA DAISY MAE!

GULP!! - AH **KNEW THET** FELLA WOULDN'T STOP! - HE HAD A **MEAN FACE!** HOPE TH' **NEXT** FELLA WILL STOP!!

THET CAR IS A-STOPPIN' FO' ME !! - WHEW!! - TH' WAY HE PUT HIS BRAKES ON, HE SHORE RAISED A TREMENJUS CLOUD O' **DUST !!**

2-4

THANK YO', SUH! - **ACHOO!!** - WHUT DUST!!

AS SOON AS AH GITS THIS DUST OUTA MAH EYES AH WILL INTERDOOCE MAHSELF TO **YO'** AN' **YO'** KIN INTERDOOCE **YO'**SELF T' **ME !!**

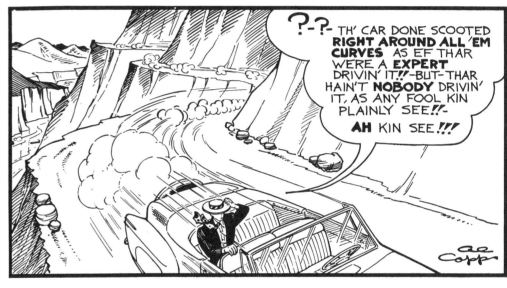

42

LI'L ABNER

by AL CAPP!!

AH DIDN'T GIVE YO' TH' RAZZBERRY, OFFICER!—TH' DRIVER DID IT!—BUT—GULP!—THAR HAIN'T NO DRIVER AS ANY FOOL KIN PLAINLY SEE! —SEE?

IF YOU DON'T STOP—I'LL SHOOT AT YOUR TIRES!!

AH IS W-WILLIN' T' STOP—BUT TH' LI'L MAN WHO ISN'T THAR—HE WON'T STOP!!

THIS IS C-CONFOOZIN' BUT NOT AMOOZIN'!!!

GULP!!—THIS IS TH' MOST UNLAWFUL CAR AH EVER RID IN—

HOLLYWOOD!—THIS SOOPERHOOMIN CAR TOOK ME JEST WHAR AH WANTED T'GO!!—IT'S ALL BIN SO CONFOOZIN'—AN'—THET BUZZIN' SOUND AH HEERD ALL 'LONG TH' TRIP—THET WERE CONFOOZIN' TOO!!

CONGRATULATIONS!—YOU WERE THE FIRST PASSENGER IN HISTORY IN A CAR DRIVEN BY REMOTE CONTROL!!

WAL, YO' SHOULDA CONTROLLED TH' RAZZ-BERRIES WHICH THIS SASSY CAR GAVE TO THET PO-LICEMAN!!

HA-HA!!—THAT WAS JUST A BIT OF HUMOR TO BRIGHTEN TH' MONOTONY!!

("A PITCHER O' HER!")

SENSATIONAL DISCOVERY IN FIRST STARRING ROLE

GLAMOURMOUNT'S NEW STARLET, MISS CHERRY BLOSSOM, STARTS HER FIRST PICTURE TODAY. ALTHOUGH ALL AMERICA IS QUIVERING WITH CURIOSITY TO SEE HER EYES, MISS BLOSSOM WILL CONTINUE TO WEAR THE HAIR-DO WHICH HAS MADE HER FAMOUS SINCE THE FIRST DAY SHE APPEARED IN HOLLYWOOD. SHE WILL EXPRESS ALL EMOTIONS BY DILATING HER NOSTRILS.

HER SET IS CLOSED TO VISITORS, AND THE STARLET IS CLOSELY GUARDED FROM ALL INQUISITIVE PERSONS...

LI'L ABNER

by AL CAPP!!

LI'L ABNER
by AL CAPP !!

Li'l ABNER
by AL CAPP!!

AH'VE LOOKED ALL OVAH TH' YEW-NITED STATES— FO' (-SOB-)-CHERRY BLOSSOM WIF TH' HEART-SHAPED EARS— BUT—(-GULP!-)-AH CAIN'T NOT FIND HER!!

TH' DOCTOR SAID EF AH DIDN'T FIND HER—AH'D LOSE MAH MIND! THET'D BE A T-TURRIBLE BLOW T'ME ON ACCOUNT TH' THING AH IS PROUDEST OF IS MAH INTELLY-JUNCE!!

R-RECKON AH BETTER G-GO BACK T' DOGPATCH AN' LOSE MAH MIND— (-GULP-)-THAR'S NO BETTER PLACE T' LOSE IT!!

2-17 818

MEANWHILE: DOGPATCH—

WAL, HYAR AH IS!— READY T' PERFORM TH' CEREMONY FO' WHICH BIG BARNSMELL PAID ME IN ADVANCE! WHAR'S DAISY MAE?

SHE DISAPPEARED 'BOUT A MONTH AGO. SHE SAID SHE'D BE A-COMIN' BACK IN A MONTH— BUT THAR HAIN'T BIN A SIGN O' HER!!

Copr. 1942 by United Feature Syndicate, Inc.
Tm. Reg. U. S. Pat. Off.—All rights reserved

DEEP IN THE HILLS NEAR DOGPATCH—

RAIN!!- TSK!- TSK!!

2-18

THERE'S A LI'L COTTAGE— MAYBE THEY'LL GIVE ME A FLOP FOR THE NIGHT!

Copr. 1942 by United Feature Syndicate, Inc.
Tm. Reg. U. S. Pat. Off.—All rights reserved
819

OH, LI'L ABNER!-IT'S A-RAININ' OUTSIDE!!— WE CAIN'T GO FO' OUR STROLL IN TH' MOON-LIGHT, AS USUAL— WE'LL HAFTA SET IN!!

YO' IS YAWNIN'!!-SLEEPY?- AH'LL FIX YO' BED, MAH SWEET HUSBIN'—

CHUCKLE!- HONEYMOONERS!! THREE WOULD BE A CROWD!!

47

LI'L ABNER

by AL CAPP!!

LI'L ABNER

by AL CAPP!!

LI'L ABNER

by AL CAPP !!

LI'L ABNER by AL CAPP!!

56

LI'L ABNER *by* AL CAPP!!

(*"I'M AFRAID MY EDITOR WAS *WRONG!!*—THERE ISN'T A *FLAW* IN HIS CHARACTER!—HE SPENDS HIS *EVERY* MOMENT DOING *INCREDIBLY KINDLY DEEDS*—AND, WORKING INCREDIBLY HARD!—THE POOR DARLING HAS *NEVER* TAKEN A VACATION!")

MR. GARK!!—I HAVE DISCOVERED *ANOTHER* ISOLATED MOUNTAIN COMMUNITY.!!

EXCELLENT!!—OF *ALL* MY PHILANTHROPIES, THE ONE I ENJOY *MOST* IS FINDING ISOLATED MOUNTAIN COMMUNITIES—AND AIDING THEM—

3-12

AH-H!—A LIST OF ITS INHABITANTS—— HM— HM—— *AH!!!*

MISS HAZARD, I THINK I WILL TAKE MY *FIRST* VACATION!—I HAVE ALWAYS WANTED TO GO ON A—ER—*HUNTING* TRIP——AND—NOW—I *WILL*—

838

CHIEF, I'VE HAD J. SWEETLIPS GARKS UNDER OBSERVATION FOR TWO WEEKS!—THAT OLD DARLING *IS* JUST AS GOOD AS HE *SEEMS* TO BE!!

HM-M!—I WOULD HAVE STAKED MY REPUTATION AS A STUDENT OF HUMAN NATURE—

THAT A MAN AS *SEEMINGLY* PERFECT AS THAT—MUST HAVE *ONE* FLAW!—BUT—I'LL HAVE TO ADMIT I WAS *WRONG!*—THE CASE IS CLOSED!

THE POOR DEAR IS OFF ON HIS *FIRST* VACATION IN TWENTY-FIVE YEARS—A LITTLE *HUNTING* TRIP.

3-13

(*CHUCKLE!*—IT GIVES ME A BOOT T' SEE THAT SWEET OLD SOUL FONDLE THAT HUNTING-RIFLE—*")

(*CHUCKLE!*—I'LL BET HE WON'T EVEN *USE* IT!—HE'S TOO *TENDER-HEARTED*--TOO *GENTLE!* CHEE!—WHEN YA COME T' THINK OF IT—HE'S KINDA LIKE A —*ANGEL!*")

AH-H!—THE OUTSKIRTS OF DOGPATCH! YOU MAY LEAVE ME *HERE*, MY BOY!!

839

LI'L ABNER
by AL CAPP!!

LI'L ABNER

by AL CAPP !!

LI'L ABNER by AL CAPP!!

JEB SCRAGG!!- TH' CROOLEST, MOST INHOOMAN O' ALL TH' SCRAGGS!

HE'S TH' BLACKSHEEP O' TH' SCRAGG FAMBLY!- AN'-THEY IS -(-GULP.!) ALL BLACKSHEEP!

Y-YO' IS GONNA SHOOT US, NATCHERLY!

OH, NO, MY DEAR HOSTS—

3-19

—I'M NOT GOING TO SHOOT YOU!!

OH, HAPPY DAY!!—HE HAIN'T GONNA SHOOT US!!

DID YO' HEAR WHUT HE SAID, PANSY?-HE HAIN'T GONNA SHOOT US!-OH, BLESS YO' SCRAWNY HIDE, JEB SCRAGG!!

DON'T BE SO HAPPY, YO' CHUCKLE-HAIDS! THAR'S MORE'N ONE WAY O' KILLIN' A YOKUM!!

Copr. 1942 by United Feature Syndicate, Inc.
Tm. Reg. U. S. Pat. Off.—All rights reserved 844

HE JEST SAID HE WARN'T GONNA SHOOT US!-WHY IS YO' SO WORRIED, MAMMY?-WHY DON'T YO' HAVE SOME FAITH IN HIM?

ON ACCOUNT HE'S A SCRAGG, THASS WHY!!

SOMEHOW, AH TRUSTS HIM!!-AH'LL BET HE WON'T SHOOT US!!

YOU WIN!!

3-20

Copr. 1942 by United Feature Syndicate, Inc.
Tm. Reg. U. S. Pat. Off.—All rights reserved 845

I'M GOING TO BLOW YOU TO KINGDOM COME!!!

AH-H!!—BARBECUED CHICKEN!-FOOD AND ENTERTAINMENT!-I'LL HAVE AN OLD-FASHIONED PICNIC—ROMAN STYLE!!

IT (-GULP.!) SHORE HAIN'T D-DOGPATCH STYLE!!

Li'l ABNER by AL CAPP!!

A HOSPITAL IN A SOUTHERN CITY—

YOU'RE PRACTICALLY RECOVERED FROM YOUR ACCIDENT, MISS DAY. ALL THAT REMAINS TO BE DONE IS TO RE-SET YOUR FACIAL FEATURES.

WAS THERE ANYTHING ABOUT YOUR FACE YOU WOULD WANT CHANGED?

YO' MEAN — YO' CAN RE-SET MAH FEATURES— ANY WAY AH WANT?

YES — I THINK I CAN!!

THERE IS A PAINTING IN THE MUSEUM CALLED "MOUNTAIN GIRL". AH WOULD RATHER LOOK LIKE THAT MAKE-BELIEVE GIRL THAN ANYONE IN THE WORLD—

HM — I THINK IT CAN BE DONE!!

TWO MONTHS ELAPSE BETWEEN THIS AND THE FOLLOWING EPISODE—

THIS WAY, GENTLEMEN.

AND — NOW I WILL PLACE MY PATIENT NEXT TO THE PAINTING— PLEASE REMOVE YOUR HAT, MY DEAR—

YES, DOCTOR.

GREAT SCOTT, DOCTOR— YOU'VE DONE IT!!

YOU HAVE ACTUALLY DUPLICATED THE BEAUTY OF THAT MAKE-BELIEVE GIRL IN THE PAINTING!!

AND — REMEMBER — THERE WAS ABSOLUTELY NO RESEMBLANCE BETWEEN MISS MAISIE DAY AND THIS IMAGINARY GIRL — EXCEPT THAT BOTH WERE ABOUT THE SAME SIZE — AND BLONDE!!

OH! — AH'M GLAD AH WAS IN THE ACCIDENT THAT MADE IT NECESSARY TO RE-SET MAH FEATURES!!

LI'L ABNER

by AL CAPP!!

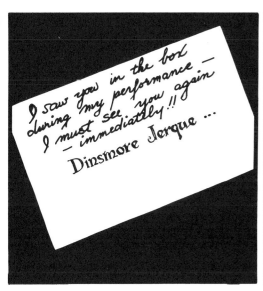

LI'L ABNER
by AL CAPP!!

LI'L ABNER

by AL CAPP!!

PORE DAISY MAE!-AH OUGHTA BE **FOORIOUS** AT HER FO' SLAPPIN' ME-BUT WHEN AH THINKS O' HOW SHE'S PROB'LY **EATIN' HER HEART OUT WIF REMORSE**-AH FEELS KINDA **SORRY** FO' HER!!

NATCHERLY, SHE'LL BE COMIN' 'ROUN'-HER EYES WET WIF TEARS-HER THROAT CHOKIN' WIF **SOBS**-T'BEG ME T' FO'GIVE HER!-O'COURSE-AH **WILL** FO'GIVE HER IN TH' END-**BUT**-FUST-AH'LL BE STERN!!

"DAISY MAE"-AH WILL SAY IN A COLD AN' MIZZUBLE VOICE-"YO' **HAS WOUNDED ME DEEPLY, AN' AH DUNNO EF AH CARES T' RESOOM FRIENDLY RE-LAY-SHUNS WIF YO'!!**" --YIPPAY! THASS A HUMDINGER!! CAIN'T HARDLY **WAIT** T'SAY IT!- WISHT SHE'D **COME!!**

MEANWHILE-

G-GOSH DAISY MAE!-YO' ALLUS USETA AVOID ME ON ACCOUNT AH IS **SO** HOMELY!!

THAR'S BIN SOME CHANGES MADE!!-NOW, TH' HOMELIER THEY IS-TH' **BETTER** AH LIKES 'EM!!

THEN **AH** IS TH' MAN FO' YO'!

(*CHUCKLE!-IT DOES MAH OLE HEART GOOD T' SEE TH' CHILE ACT SO **DIFF'RUNT!**-SHE'S BIN A-PLAYIN' "**POST OFFICE**" WIF THESE BOYS ALL EVENIN'!!- AT THIS RATE, SHE'LL TRAP HERSELF A HUSBIN' IN **JIG** TIME-")

ANOTHER KISS?--**SHO' 'NUFF!!**

THAR SHO' **HAS** BIN SOME CHANGES MADE!-SHE USETA RUN AFTER **LI'L ABNER** ALL TH' TIME!

NOW SHE SAYS EF HE SHOWS HIS HAN'SOME FACE 'ROUN' HYAR AGIN, SHE'LL SMACK IT!!

"NO USE A-MOANIN' AN' A-GROANIN'-NO USE A-SOBBIN' AN' A-THROBBIN'!!-YO' HAS ACTED **VURRY PEEKOOLYAR** T' ME LATELY, DAISY MAE, SO AH IS PUNISHIN' YO' BY REFOOZIN' T' REZOOM FRIENDLY RELAYSHUNS"

MOO!!

MY!-AH HAS WORKED UP SOME **FINE** SPEECHES T' USE ON DAISY MAE WHEN SHE COMES BEGGIN' ME T' FO'GIVE HER!!- PORE SOUL-SHE'S PROB'LY **AFEERD** T' COME HYAR!!- AH'LL BE NOBLE!!-AH'LL GO THAR!!!

AH'LL BE A GENNULMAN! AH'LL GO REMIND DAISY MAE IT'S TIME SHE CAME T' PLEAD WIF ME T' FO'GIVE HER!-AH HAS WORKED OUT SEV'RAL FINE SPEECHES **REFOOZIN'** T'DO IT!!

THE OFFICES OF AVAILABLE JONES-

BUT AH IS YO' OWN COUSIN, NAME OF 'DISGUSTIN' JONES, AN'AH IS MATREE-MONIALLY INCLINED!-HASN'T YO' GOT EVEN **ONE** GAL AVAILABLE, AVAILABLE?

NOT FO' YO'!!-YO' IS TOO DISGUSTIN', DISGUSTIN'!!

MY MOTTO: I'LL DO ANY-THING FOR A PRICE!!

MAH BUSINESS REPOOTAYSHUN WOULD BE **ROONED** EF AH GAVE MAH SEAL OF APPROVAL TO ANYONE AS DISGUSTIN' AS **YO'** IS, DISGUSTIN'!!

THEN-(*GULP!*) YOUR FINAL WORD IS—YO' HAIN'T GOT NOTHIN' AVAILABLE, HUH, AVAILABLE?

RIGHT!!-EF YO' WAS AS HANSOME AS LI'L ABNER THAR-**ANY** GAL WOULD BE HAPPY T' BE WOOED BY YO'. NOT ONLY IS HE HAN'SOME, BUT HE'S GOT **TECK-NEEK!!**

AH DOUBTS EF AH WILL EVAH BE AS HAN'SOME AS HIM—BUT AH KIN STUDY HIS **TECK-NEEK!** AH'LL FOLLY HIM —SECRUTLY!!

AND SO, DISGUSTIN' JONES WALKS INTO HIS GREATEST ADVENTURE!!!

("AH MAY NEVAH BE TH' GLAMMER BOY **HE** IS-BUT-AH KIN STUDY UP ON HIS **TECK-NEEK**. MIGHTY CONVENIENT THET HE TALKS TO HISSELF OUT LOUD!")

DAISY MAE! YO' KIN STOP SOBBIN' NOW AN' GIT UP OFF YO' KNEES!

AH **ACCEPTS** YO' APOLOGY FO' SLAPPIN' ME-BUT SEE THET IT DON'T HAPPEN **AGIN!!**

OH, WHUT FORCEFUL TONES—WHUT MASTERFUL WORDS—WHUT TECK-NEEK!

DAISY MAE!!-AH HAS DECIDED T'ALLOW YO' T'AX MAH FORGIVENESS!-YO' MAY NOW DO WHUT YO' HAS BEEN **YEARNIN'** T' DO!!

THANK YO'!

SMASH!!

GULP!!

Li'L ABNER
by AL CAPP!!

LI'L ABNER by AL CAPP !!

A HOSPITAL NEAR PINEAPPLE JUNCTION—

YOU'RE COMPLETELY WELL NOW, MR. JERQUE, AFTER THE SMASH-UP WHICH KEPT YOU HOSPITALIZED ALL THESE WEEKS!

THROUGH IT ALL, YOU REMAINED FAITHFULLY AT MY SIDE, MAISIE DAY!!

("HM!—HE HAIN'T COMPLETELY CURED!—HE CALLS ME MAISIE DAY—SO HE STILL GOT A IMPEDIMENT IN HIS SPEECH—BUT IT MIGHT HURT HIS FEELINS EF AH MENSHUNS IT!")

WE WERE ON OUR WAY TO THE PREACHER'S WHEN THE ACCIDENT HAPPENED!—WE'LL GET THERE THIS TIME!!

Y-YES--- ("DUNNO WHUFFO' HE WANTS T'GO T'TH' PREACHERS—BUT HE'S SO PURTY, AH CAIN'T REFOOZE T'DO ANYTHING HE WISHES!")

Copr. 1942 by United Feature Syndicate, Inc.
Tm. Reg. U. S. Pat. Off.—All rights reserved
4-21

MARRIAGES PERFORMED WHILE YOU WAIT! LOWEST RATES —NO TIPPING!

("J-JEST EE-MAGINE !!—ME DISGUSTIN' JONES, ABOUT TO WED A REAL HOOMIN GAL!")

ME AN' THIS LI'L CRITTER WISHES T' COMMIT MARRIAGE!

ANOTHER COUPLE CAME IN BEFORE YO'—MAH WIFE AN' BOY USUALLY SERVE AS WITNESSES—BUT THEY'RE GONE. PERHAPS BOTH YOU YOUNG COUPLES CAN SERVE AS WITNESSES AT EACH OTHERS' WEDDINGS!!

Copr. 1943 by United Feature Syndicate, Inc.
Tm. Reg. U. S. Pat. Off.—All rights reserved
4-22

THEY'RE WILLING—ARE YOU?

OF COURSE!

("?-?-?- WONDER WHY HE BRANG ME HYAR!—WONDER WHUT THEY IS TALKIN' 'BOUT!")

THIS WAY, PLEASE !!!!

AND IF YOU THINK YOU KNOW WHAT'S GOING TO HAPPEN—YOU'RE WRONG!!

74

Li'l ABNER

by AL CAPP !!

Li'L ABNER

by AL CAPP!!

THE BLACK-OUT CONTINUES—

AND NOW TWO OF YOU ARE MAN AND WIFE!

W-WHICH TWO?

POPPA!!—MOMMA AND I SAW A CUSTOMER'S CAR PARKED OUTSIDE!—DO YOU NEED **US** AS WITNESSES?

WE'VE BEEN GETTING ALONG **FINE**, SON!—**ONE** OF THESE YOUNG COUPLES SERVED AS WITNESSES FOR THE **OTHER'S** WEDDING—BUT NOW THAT **YOU** TWO ARE HERE—**THE YOUNG COUPLE WHO WERE JUST MARRIED CAN LEAVE**—

LET'S GO, DEAR—

THE LIGHTS ARE ON AGAIN!!—AND NOW I WILL MARRY YOU TWO LOVE-BIRDS!!

B-BUT **YO'** IS **DISGUSTIN'!**

YO' SAID IT, HONEY—BUT, LE'S SKIP TH' LOVE-MAKIN' TILL TH' CEREMONY IS OVAH. PROCEED, PREACHER!!

DIDN'T YO' **HEAR** ME, MISS?—AH SAID—IS YO' **WILLIN'** T' TAKE THIS LI'L CRITTER FO' YO' **LAWFUL WEDDED HUSBIN?**

WHY IS YO' LOOKIN' AT ME THET **WAY?**—DON'T YO' **KNOW ME?** AH IS **DISGUSTIN'.**

YO' **SHORE IS!!**

OH, WHAR IS THET **PURTY** FELLA AH CAME **IN** WIF!

GOOD HEAVENS!!—IN THE CONFUSION O' TH' BLACKOUT—AH MARRIED TH' **WRONG** PEOPLE!!

YO' **HAIN'T** GONNA MARRY WIF ME?—OH (—SOB—)—YO' HAIN'T TH' GAL AH **THOUGHT** YO' WERE!

YO' NEVAH SPOKE A **TRUER** WORD!!

GULP!—AH'VE **LOST** HER!—OH—EF ONLY AH HAD MAH LIFE T' LIVE **OVER** AGIN—AH'D GRAB HER IN MAH ARMS—T' TELL HER AH **LOVES** HER—AN'—THEN **AH'D MARRY WIF HER!!**—YES—**THASS** WHUT AH'D DO—AH'D **MARRY WIF HER!!**

LI'L ABNER

by AL CAPP!!

OH!—EF ONLY AH'D **ONE MO' CHANCE!!**—AH WOULDN'T OF LET **NO ONE ELSE GET HER**—AH'D OF MARRIED WIF HER **PERSONALLY**—Y-YES—THASS WHUT AH'D OF DONE!!!

YO' **HAS** ONE MO' **CHANCE!!**—YO' **KIN** MARRY WIF ME **PERSONALLY!!!!**—OH, HAIN'T YO' **HAPPY**?

NO ONE ELSE C'D EVAH GIT ME, LI'L ABNER—JEST **YO**'—FUM TH' FUST DAY AH SEEN YO'—AH KNEW AH HAD T' B'LONG T' **YO**'—AN' T' **NOBODY ELSE**—

AH- HAS BIN READY T' BE Y-YORN—ANY TIME YO' WANTED ME—AN'—NOW—THET TIME HAS **COME**—AH KIN SEE THET—BY TH' EXPRESSION ON YO' **FACE**—

YO' IS LOOKIN' AT ME WIF AN' EXPRESSION AH NEVAH **SEEN** BEFO'—IT'S **LOVE**, LI'L ABNER—JEST P-PLAIN **L-LOVE!!**—TH' MINUTE AH'VE BIN WAITIN' FO'—ALL MAH LIFE—IT'S **COME!!**—YO' IS ABOUT T' **AX** ME T' BE YORN!!

GO ON, YO' BIG LUNK-HAID—AX HER!!

AN' SLIP HER A LI'L KISS, TOO!—WHOOP IT UP!—MAKE IT **REAL** ROMANTICAL!

MOON-BEAM McSWINE!!

CAIN'T UNNERSTAN' **WHY** HE RUN AWAY AFTER AH GAVE HIM ALL THET ENCOURAGEMENT!!

YOU **FOOL**!!—IT ✷SOB✷ WERE TH' **FIRST TIME** IN HIS LIFE HE D-DIDN'T ✷SOB✷ NEED ANY!!—YO' DONE BROKE TH' S-SPELL!!

77

LI'L ABNER

by AL CAPP!!

SOMEHOW—AH NEVAH THINKS O' SALOMEY AS BEIN' ANY DIFF'RUNT FUM US!

THAR HAINT MUCH DIFF'RUNCE, MOST FOLKS SAY!

THAR DO SEEM T'BE SOMETHIN' ABOUT SALOMEY THET'S SUPERIOR T'OTHER PIGS!!

THASS RIGHT MAMMY— SHE'S A PEARL AMONG SWINE

MEBBE SHE JEST SEEMS DIFF'RUNT T'US ON ACCOUNT WE LOVES HER SO.

MEBBE T'OTHER FOLKS SHE'D SEEM LIKE A ORDINARY PIG!!

4-30

PASSING THROUGH THE HILLS IS THE GREAT SPORTSMAN PIG-BREEDER J.P. FANGSBY.

GREAT SCOTT!! IT CAN'T BE!!— YES! IT IS!!

HOG-LOVERS' GUIDE

THE ONLY LIVING FEMALE OF THE SPECIES "HAMMUS ALABAMMUS" WITH A ZOOT SNOOT AND A DRAPE SHAPE!!

STOP THE CAR, GAYLORD!!

THE PRINCELY CARAVAN OF THE WORLD'S GREATEST SPORTSMAN HOG-BREEDER, J.P. FANGSBY, COMES TO A SUDDEN STOP IN THE HILLS!!

BOAR SCARLOFF

5-1

STOP SQUIRMING, BLAST YOU!!

I'VE FOUND IT AT LAST! THE ONLY LIVING FEMALE OF THE SPECIES "HAMMUS ALABAMMUS" WITH A ZOOT SNOOT AND A DRAPE SHAPE!!

881

AND—BY A STROKE OF GOOD FORTUNE—I OWN THE ONLY LIVING MALE OF THE SPECIES!!—I HAVE FOUND A MATE FOR YOU, BOAR SCARLOFF!!

BOAR SCARLOFF

LI'L ABNER by AL CAPP !!

WHAT A FANTASTIC STROKE OF GOOD FORTUNE !! TO FIND THE ONLY LIVING FEMALE OF THE "HAMMUS ALABAMMUS" SPECIES **RUNNING WILD** IN THESE HILLS !!

ALL MY LIFE I'VE WANTED TO BREED THE "HAMMUS ALABAMMUS" SPECIES !— AND NOW— I HAVE **BOTH** A **MALE** AND A **FEMALE** !!— THEY'LL MAKE THE SWEETEST COUPLE !!—

THIS HAS BEEN A HAPPY DAY FOR ALL OF US—!

STEP ON THE GAS, GAYLORD !!

CAIN'T FIND MAH LI'L **SUGAR PLUM** ANYWHAR! —NOTHIN' LEFT T'DO BUT T'CONJURE UP A VISION !!

(—"GULP!—A VISION! AH'M A GONER!—")

TURNIPS
KEEP OUT

FUST AH MARKS A "X" ON MAH BROW WIF FRESH BLOOD DRAWED FUM A INNOCENT LAMB!

IT'S MIGHTY NICE O' YO' T'SAY THET, MAMMY!

AH WHIRLS AROUN' THREE TIMES, REPEATIN' TH' MAGICAL WORDS MAH GRAN'MAMMY TEACHED ME!—THEN AH LAYS STIFF AN' STILL !! TH' VISION'S COMIN'!

(—"IT **IS!** GULP! THEN AH MIGHT'S WELL GIVE MAHSELF UP!!") HYAR AH IS, PANSY!

HMPH!—AH KNOWED **YO'** WAS IN THET BARR'L ALL TH' TIME, YO' LI'L VARMINT! MAH LI'L **SUGAR PLUM** IS **SALOMEY!**—AN' S-SHE IS IN (GULP!)— **DANGER !!**

LI'L ABNER by AL CAPP!!

80

LI'L ABNER

by AL CAPP!!

BUT, MADAME, **WHY** DID YOU PUNCH ME IN THE BELLY? ALL I WANT TO DO IS MARRY **YOUR** PIG TO **MINE**. I OFFERED YOU $500 FOR IT. WASN'T THAT **ENOUGH**?

-A **BILLION** WOULDN'T BE ENOUGH- NOR EVEN A **MILLION**!!

SALOMEY IS LIKE OUR **OWN DOTTER**! -WE'VE BRUNG HER UP **TENDERLY**- ALLUS PERTECTIN' HER FUM TH' WICKEDNESS O' THE WORLD!!

SHE GOT TH' SAME IDEALS WE HAS! -MARRY HER UP T' THET LOW-CLASS, UNREFINED HAWG?- **NEVAH**!! AH BIDS YO' GOOD DAY, MR. FANGSBY, YO' MONSTER!!

(-"THAT ILLITERATE PEASANT WILL **NOT** STAND IN MY WAY!"-I'LL GET THAT FEMALE "HAMMUS ALABAMMUS" BY FAIR MEANS OR FOUL- **BUT I'LL GET IT!!**"-)

LARDLY MANOR

CHEER UP, BOAR SCARLOFF!! THAT IGNORANT PEASANT WOMAN REFUSED TO SELL ME HER LITTLE PORKER-BUT I'LL GET IT **SOMEHOW**!!- I'M OFF TO DOGPATCH NOW!-

THE NEXT DAY-DOGPATCH-

THE YOKUM FAMBLY?- AH KNOWS 'EM WELL! **PANSY** YOKUM IS TH' **STRONGEST** CHARACTER IN ALL THESE HILLS-AN' LI'L ABNER IS JEST **LIKE** HER!!

5-11

BUT-PAPPY YOKUM!! HYAW! HYAW!-A **WEAKER** CHARACTER THAR NEVAH WAS!! HE'S JEST LIKE A **CHILD**! YASSUH!!-NEVAH SEEN A GROWN MAN ANY MORE **CHILDISH** THAN HIM!! HYAW! HYAW!!

HYAR'S YO' PAPER DOLL CUT-OUTS, FANTASTIC. THEY JUST ARRIVED!

OH **HAPPY DAY**!- EXCOOZE ME-AH GOTTA GO FIND SOME SCISSORS!!

SO **PAPPY** YOKUM IS THE WEAK LINK!-I MUST WORK THROUGH HIM!!

U.S. MAI

GIVE TO THE U.S.O.

LI'L ABNER by AL CAPP !!

LI'L ABNER

by AL CAPP!!

LI'L ABNER

by AL CAPP!!

WE GOTTA GIT T' SAN ANTONE, TEXAS, PRONTO!!

WE NEEDS A BIG POW'FUL CAR T'GIT THAR, CHILLUN!

THAR'S ONE, PAPPY DEAR!!

I'M STUCK IN THE MUD. I NEED SOMETHING BIG AND SOLID TO PLACE UNDER THE WHEELS FOR TRACTION. DO YOU BOYS KNOW WHERE I CAN FIND SUCH AN OBJECT?

WE SHORE DO!!

SAN ANTONE, TEXAS— HYAR WE COME!!!

WHILE THE SCRAGGS ARE STREAKING ON TO SAN ANTONIO—

IT'S SHORTER THIS WAY, PAPPY DEAR!

KEERFUL NOT T'GIT HURT BY TH' FLYING CARCASSES, CHILLUN!!

THE YOKUMS—

SORRY WE CAIN'T STOP T' MAKE CHIN-MOOSIC WIF YO' STRANGER!

WE GOTTA GIT T' SAN ANTONE, TEXAS —BY AUTY-MOBILE!

BUT—THAT'S A WHALE OF A TRIP! DO YOU THINK YOUR TIRES WILL STAND UP ALL THAT TIME?

HM—AH RECKON THEY WILL—UNLESS TH' MICE KNOCKS 'EM OVER!—AH'LL LOCK TH' DOOR T' MAKE SHORE!!

YOU MEAN YOU'RE GOING TO RIDE ON THE RIMS?

NATCHERLY!

BUT HOW ABOUT GASOLINE RATIONING?

?—?—WHUT'S GASOLINE?

THAT'S THE STUFF THAT MAKES A CAR GO!!

HAIN'T TH' STUFF THET MAKES OUR CAR GO! WE MERELY TOSSES IN A MESS O' CORN LEAVIN'S AN' STRONG COFFEE —AN' LETS 'ER RIP!!

Li'L ABNER by AL CAPP!!

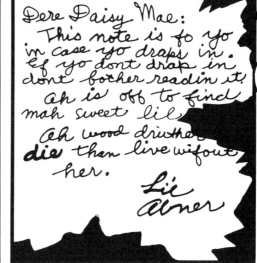

LI'L ABNER

by AL CAPP!!

WE'VE SHORE DRIVEN LIKE **FEENDS** TODAY. RECKON WE'VE DONE ALL O' THIRTY MILES! 'BOUT TIME T' REST UP, HAINT IT?—

THET **LOOKS** LIKE A PARKIN' LOT. LE'S **WAKE** LI'L ABNER AN' AX **HIM** T'READ TH' SIGN.

CASH PAID FOR JUNK

WHY BOTHER T'WAKE TH' CHILE?—LE'S USE **OUR** INTELLY-GUNCE! LOOKIT ALL THEM **OTHER** FINE CARS PARKED THAR. IT **MUST** BE A PARKIN' LOT, AS ANY FOOL KIN PLAINLY SEE! **SEE?**

(GULP!) AH SEE!

HOW MUCH?

(—HM—IT'S IN PRETTY BAD SHAPE EVEN FOR JUNK!—) OH—LET'S SAY **THIRTY-FIVE CENTS!!**

THET'S A **HEAP O' MONEY!**

GLAD YOU THINK SO— **HERE!!**

(—THIS IS A **WONDIFUL** PARKIN' LOT! **THEY** PAYS **US!**—)

HERE!—SIGN THIS—AND THEN DRAG IT INTO THE LOT!—

AH'LL SIGN IT WIF A "X" ON ACCOUNT THASS ALL TH' WRITIN' AH KNOWS.

BILL OF SALE

THIS IS A **WONDIFUL** PARKIN' LOT, HAINT IT PANSY?— **THEY** PAYS **US** FO' PARKIN' IT HYAR!

REAL **HORSPITALITY**, AH CALLS IT!—WAL (YAWN!)— LE'S GIT SOME SLEEP!!

MEANWHILE: IN THE FRONT OFFICE

I'LL BUY YOUR **WHOLE YARDFUL** OF JUNK—AT **3 CENTS A POUND!!**

IT'S A **DEAL!**—WE CAN WEIGH IT ALL, RIGHT NOW!

HOURS LATER—

THAT'S THE LAST CAR! HM!—IT WEIGHS **400** POUNDS MORE THAN I WOULD HAVE ESTIMATED!

THEY CERTAINLY BUILT CARS **SOLIDLY** IN THE OLD DAYS!!—WELL—**EVERYTHING** IN THIS YARD IS MINE NOW—BOUGHT AND PAID FOR!!

Li'l Abner by Al Capp!!

LI'L ABNER

by AL CAPP!!

Dear Mr. Fangsby:—

We is havin this letter writ by a educated varmint. We will get Salomey for 'yo' right soon on account we is already half-way to San Antonio, Texas.

We had to kill 8 or 9 fellas — we don't remember the exact amount — and also we had to steal a car to get here. Don't be afraid that this educated varmint will squeal on us. He don't know it, but, as soon as he finishes writing this letter for 'us, we is going to shoot him through the head.

yours truly
the Scraggs

Li'l ABNER *by* AL CAPP!!

A LONESOME COASTAL BEACH···

(SIGH!) THET NEWLY LAUNCHED SHIP AH STARTED OFF IN, SPRANG A LEAK, AN' TH' COAST GUARD BOAT WHICH RESCUED ME WAS SANK BY A ICE-BERG. NO SOONER DID AH CRAWL ONTO TH' ICEBERG THAN THET WERE SMASHED INTO A MILLION BITS BY A **FALLIN' METEOR!!**

YES, FOLKS—IT'S JOE BTFSPLK!! THE WORLD'S GREATEST **JINX!!**—FROM HIM COMES NOTHING BUT TROUBLE! HE SHOULDN'T HAPPEN **TO A DOG!!**

HOME AGIN! WAL-AH SPENT A VERY INJOYABLE WINTER WIF HITLER IN RUSSIA!

AN'—THEN AH VISITED A SPELL WIF MUSSOLINI'S NAVY!!—AH CAME BACK T'SEE HOW MAH FRIENDS TH' **YOKUMS** IS GITTIN' ALONG—AN' **THEN** AH HAS A DATE IN **TOKIO!!**

6-11

THEY **NEEDS** ME THAR!!

HM!—**THIS** TIRE MUSTA HIT A FELLA WIF FALSE TEETH—ON ACCOUNT THEY IS STILL A-BITIN' INTO TH' RUBBER!

THAR MUSTA BIN A RED-HOT STOVE IN TH' LAST HOUSE WE TOOK A SHORT-CUT THROUGH. **THIS** TIRE IS MOST BURNED OFF!

OH, WAL—WE GOT 200 MILES OUT OF 'EM! WHUT **MORE** KIN YO' EXPECT FUM **BRAND-NEW TIRES!**—HM! **AH GOTTA GREAT IDEA!**

SEE!—WE RIDES TH' **RIMS** ON THESE TRACKS!—WE DON'T EVEN HAFTA STEER—IN FACK—WE KIN GO T'SLEEP!

YO' GOT A FINE MIND, PAPPY DEAR!

6-12

NOW WE KIN REST WHILE WE HEADS WEST.

HO-HUM! AH SHORE FEELS HAPPY, PAPPY!

AH WANTS T'SLEEP! **LESS NOISE, BOYS!!**

CRASH!!

Li'l ABNER
by AL CAPP!!

LI'L ABNER by AL CAPP !!

LI'L ABNER by AL CAPP!!

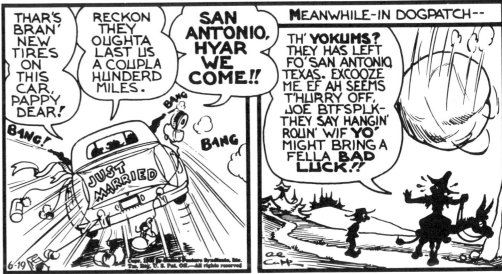

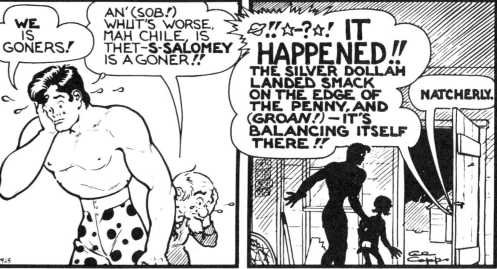

Li'l ABNER

by AL CAPP !!

LI'L ABNER by AL CAPP!!

CUSS IT! WE SEEM T'BE FOLLOWED BY A **JINX**, PAPPY DEAR!

UGH! CAIN'T MOVE THIS TREE NOHOW!

SHECKS!—LE'S **LEAVE** THIS CAR AN' GIT ANOTHER, IN TH' **USUAL MANNER!!**

HOURS LATER—

LOOK!!—THET BOOTIFUL CAR GOT A SIGN ON IT "**30 DAYS FREE TRIAL!**"

LE'S **ACCEPT** TH' OFFER!!—IT'LL BE JEST TH' FLIP OF A BICEP T' REMOVE THET TREE!!

6-27

MEANWHILE: IN THE TRUNK OF THE LIMOUSINE IS **JOE BTFSPLK**—LITTLE REALIZING THAT THE CAR HAS CHANGED OWNERS—

(CHUCKLE!) AH SHORE IS BRINGIN' MISERY T' TH' **FEENDS** A-DRIVIN' THIS CAR!—TH' YOKUMS WILL APPRESHEEATE MAH WORK, NO DOUBT!!

NOT FAR AWAY—**JAILBREAK!**

THEY THOUGHT THEY COULD KEEP **ME** PENNED UP FOR LIFE—ME—**TILLY THE KID!!**

WHRR

HAVING STARTED OUT WITH THE SCRAGGS, JOE BTFSPLK, (WORLD'S WORST **JINX**) DOESN'T REALIZE THAT THE POSSESSION OF THE CAR HAS CHANGED—

CHUCKLE!

LI'L DO THOSE FEENDS IN FRONT KNOW WHUT **BAD LUCK** IS IN STORE FO' 'EM!!

THE WORST LUCK!—TILLY THE KID—LIFE-TERMER—HAS JUST BROKEN JAIL—

STOP THAT CAR!!

YAS'M!!

6-29

WHEEE

A POLICE SIREN!!—THEY'RE BOUND TO GET ME!!

(GULP!) AH WISHES THEY'D BE A LI'L QUIETER! MAMMY AN' PAPPY IS ASLEEP IN BACK—

BUT—BEFORE THEY DO GET ME—I'M GOING TO HAVE ONE LAST FLING AT ROMANCE, BUD!!

Y-YO' IS?—

Li'l ABNER by AL CAPP!!

LI'L ABNER

by AL CAPP!!

LI'L ABNER by AL CAPP!!

Li'L ABNER by AL CAPP!!

Panel 1: BUT—?—?—WHUFFO' IS YO' WEEPIN', FANGSBY?—DIDN'T WE GIT YO' SALOMEY—ONLY LIVIN' **FEMALE** O'TH' "HAMMUS ALABAMMUS" SPECIES?

YES—SOB!—BUT—TO CELEBRATE YOUR GREAT ACHIEVEMENT— **YOU BARBECUED BOAR SCARLOFF —THE ONLY LIVING MALE!!**

OH, WELL—THE HARM IS DONE!—THIS FEMALE IS OF NO USE TO ME NOW!—I'LL MAKE THE GRANDEST GESTURE ANY HOG-BREEDER **EVER** MADE!!—

7-16

Copr. 1942 by United Features Syndicate, Inc.
Tm. Reg. U. S. Pat. Off.—All rights reserved

Panel 2: I'LL INVITE EVERY HOG-BREEDER IN THIS COUNTY TO A BANQUET!! AND THE MAIN DISH WILL BE THE RAREST OF ALL DELICACIES— **"BARBECUED FEMALE HAMMUS ALABAMMUS!!"** —AFTER THAT FEAST, THE SPECIES WILL BE **EXTINCT!!** WILL YOU GENTLEMEN PREPARE THE BARBECUE!?

SHO' NUFF!!

Panel 3: FELLOW HOG-BREEDERS!—WE ARE ABOUT TO PARTAKE OF THE LAST FEAST OF ITS KIND ON EARTH— **"BARBECUED FEMALE HAMMUS ALABAMMUS!"** AFTER WE'VE EATEN THE LAST TASTY MORSEL, THE SPECIES WILL BE **FOREVER EXTINCT!!** — I WILL NOW TAKE THE FEMALE "HAMMUS ALABAMMUS" TO THE BARBECUERS, AWAITING IN THE CELLAR—

7-17

Copr. 1942 by United Features Syndicate, Inc.
Tm. Reg. U. S. Pat. Off.—All rights reserved

Panel 4: ONE HOUR LATER—

DELICIOUS!

SO JUICY!

SO TENDER!

URP!

TOO BAD FANGSBY NEVER **DID** COME UP FROM THE CELLAR!

WONDER WHAT KEPT HIM DOWN THERE!

LOOK, PAPPY! **THAR'S SALOMEY!**

BUT—?—?— AH THOUGHT WE'D BARBECUED HER!!

IT WERE POW'FUL DARK WHEN FANGSBY BRANG HER DOWN! —HM!—AH KNOWS WE BARBECUED **SOMETHIN'!**

LI'L ABNER
by AL CAPP!!

(SOB!) IT'S NO USE PLACIN' THET VACANT CHAIR AT TH' TABLE - AN' A-SETTIN' SALOMEY'S FAVORITE DISHES IN FRONT O' IT. IT'S - N-NO--USE PERTENDIN'! - SHE J-JEST -HAINT --THAR!!

AN' N-**NEVAH** WILL BE- N-NEVAH AGIN!!

OH, (SOB!) -SHE WERE A PEARL AMONG SWINE!

OINK!

WE DON'T KNOW **HOW** YO' GOT HOME, SALOMEY-

BUT HOME YO' **IS** -AN' HOME YO' **STAYS!**

-TILL DEATH DO US PART!

-AND-SPEAKING OF DEATH - THERE'S AN ABANDONED CABIN NEARBY - AND, IN IT -**AN ACCURSED CLOCK !!**

AH!-THERE'S AN' INTERESTING OLD SHACK!-WONDER IF THERE ARE ANY **ANTIQUES** IN IT—

THROUGH THE WINDOW I SAW WHAT LOOKED LIKE THE RAREST OF **ALL** OLD AMERICAN PIECES -**A REAL GRANDPAPPY'S CLOCK!!**- THERE DOESN'T SEEM TO BE ANYONE AT HOME- AND -THE DOOR- IS **OPEN** - - -

DON'T GO IN THAR, STRANGER!!!- AN' YO' SHORE **MUST** BE A STRANGER -OR YOU WOULDN'T **DAST** GO IN THAR!!

BUT, **MADAM**- THIS HOUSE IS **UNPROTECTED** -AND THERE'S A **VERY VALUABLE CLOCK INSIDE**-

STRANGER!-THET CLOCK IS AS **SAFE AS EF** IT WERE PROTECTED BY TH' WHOLE **YEW-NITED STATES ARMY!!** THET CLOCK- -**BRR-R!!**

7-20

Li'l ABNER by AL CAPP!!

THET CLOCK, STRANGER - GOT A **CURSE** ON IT!! - Y'ARS AGO YOUNG YANCEY WERE A-GOIN' T' MARRY TH' MOST BOOTIFUL GAL IN ALL THESE HILLS!!

HIM AN' TH' PREACHER WERE WAITIN' **RIGHT IN THAR.** THE BRIDE-T'-BE WAS S'POSED T' ARRIVE **SOON'S** TH' OLE CLOCK STRUCK TWELVE - 'TWERE FIXED SO THET AT TH' **STROKE O' TWELVE** IT'D CHIME OUT "TH' WEDDIN' MARCH"!!

7-21

WAL - TH' CLOCK **STRUCK TWELVE** AN' THEN COME TH' NEWS THET **TH' BOOTIFUL BRIDE-T'-BE DONE RAN OFF WIF ANOTHER MAN!** - THEN YOUNG YANCEY **RIPPED OUT WIF HIS CURSE!!** - IT WERE AS FOLLOWS -

Copr. 1942 by United Feature Syndicate, Inc.
Tm. Reg. U. S. Pat. Off.—All rights reserved

- THET AT TH' STROKE O' **TWELVE** THET CLOCK WOULD **FO'EVAH** AFTER CHIME OUT TH' **FOONERAL MARCH** - AN' THET TH' **MOST BOOTIFUL GAL** WHO HAPPENED T' BE NEAR THET CLOCK - **WOULD BE MURDERED!!!**

AND, D-DID THE CURSE COME **TRUE?**

NATCHERLY!

YES, STRANGER! - THET OLE CLOCK GOT "**YOUNG YANCEY'S CURSE**" ON IT!! - EV'RY TIME IT STRIKES MIDNIGHT IT CHIMES OUT TH' FOONERAL MARCH - AN' TH' MOST BOOTIFUL GAL WHICH HAPPENS T' BE IN TH' HOUSE IS MURDERED!!

YOU DON'T **REALLY** BELIEVE THAT, DO YOU?

WE DIDN'T AT **FIRST,** STRANGER! - FOLKS KEP' MOVIN' INTO THET HOUSE WIF TH' CLOCK IN IT, BUT - BR-RR!! - WE B'LIEVES IT **NOW!** - TH' CARCASSES O' THREE BOOTIFUL YOUNG GALS DONE CONVINCED US!!

AND SO - BECAUSE OF THAT **SILLY** SUPERSTITION THE HOUSE IS DESERTED - AND **ANYONE** CAN TAKE THAT CLOCK, EH?

ANYONE **FOOLISH** 'NUFF COULD TAKE IT - BUT THET CUSSED OBJECK WOULDN'T GIT HOUSE ROOM WIF NOBODY IN **MAH FAMBLY!!**

(*HM!* - I KNOW **JUST** THE PERSON TO SELL THIS CLOCK TO - SHE'S **MAD** ABOUT EARLY AMERICANA!*)

7-22

A LONG-DISTANCE CALL TO PARK AVENUE, N.Y.

YES!! - THIS IS BESSIE BOPSHIRE!! - A **REAL** GRAND-PAPPY CLOCK!! - WITH A **CURSE** ON IT!! - HOW **DELIGHTFUL!** - AND YOU THINK YOU CAN GET IT FOR ONLY **TEN THOUSAND DOLLARS!** - SHIP IT TO ME - AT **ONCE!!!**

Copr. 1942 by United Feature Syndicate, Inc.
Tm. Reg. U. S. Pat. Off.—All rights reserved

LI'L ABNER

by AL CAPP !!

NOW, AH REMEMBERS WHUT WERE IN THOSE RAGS IN BACK! — OH, WAL, 'TWARN'T NOTHIN' **VALOOBLE**!!

8-1

MOONBEAM McSWINE!

Copr. 1942 by United Feature Syndicate, Inc.
Tm. Reg. U. S. Pat. Off.—All rights reserved

AH IS GOIN' T'MAH AUNT BESSIE'S IN **NOO YAWK**!! AH HAINT GOT 'NOUGH GAS T'TAKE YO' BACK!!

THASS ALL RIGHT! AH'LL GO WIF YO'! AH WON'T BE NO TROUBLE T'YO' AUNT. AH'LL SLEEP WIF TH' HAWGS!!

SHE DON'T HAVE HAWGS!!

POOR, HUH?

HYAR'S MAH AUNT BESSIE'S HOUSE, MOONBEAM McSWINE!! ALL AH GOTTA DO T'FIX HER "GRAN'PAPPY CLOCK" IS WIND IT WIF THIS LI'L KEY. THAR HAINT ANOTHER ONE LIKE IT IN TH' WORLD—OOPS!

BENITO!! GIVA DA MAN BACK HEESA KEY!!

ADOLFO AND HIS MONKEY BENITO

A FEW MINUTES LATER—

SEE!—BENITO NO STEAL KEY! HE LEAVE IT ON WINDOW LEDGE—AN' NOW, HE COME-A DOWN! GOOD LI'L BENITO!—HE NEVER KEEP NOTHIN' FOR HIMSELF!!

AH'LL GO INTO TH' BUILDIN' AN' AX 'EM EF AH KIN GIT TH' KEY!

BUT, MA'M—ALL AH WANTS T'DO IS GO INTO THIS BUILDIN' AN' GIT—

THERE'S NOTHING **YOU** CAN GET IN THIS BUILDING!!—THIS IS "THE BACHELOR GIRLS' EXCLUSIVE HOTEL!" NO MEN ALLOWED—GOOD **DAY**, SIR!!—

8-3

Copr. 1942 by United Feature Syndicate, Inc.
Tm. Reg. U. S. Pat. Off.—All rights reserved

119

LI'L ABNER
by AL CAPP !!

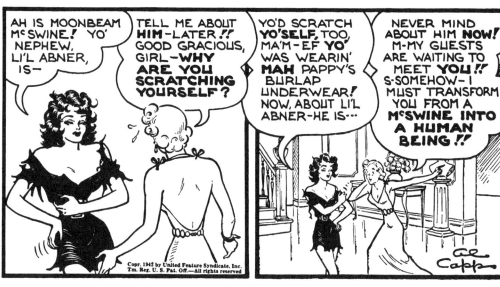

LI'L ABNER by AL CAPP!!

Li'l ABNER

by AL CAPP !!

TH' MOST BOOTIFUL GAL IN THIS ROOM IS GONNA BE M-MURDERED! OH, PERTECT ME, LI'L ABNER !!— AH DON'T WANNA DIE.!!

C-CLING T'ME, MOON-BEAM!

THIS IS ME —AUNT BESSIE! THERE'S SOMEONE ELSE IN THIS ROOM! SOMEONE WHO WASN'T HERE WHEN TH' LIGHTS WENT OUT!!

BLURP!

AH GOT YO !!

BLURP BLURP!

I FOUND THE LIGHT SWITCH! WHOM HAVE YOU THERE?

TH' MURDERER!! AH WERE ABLE T'FIND HIM IN TH' DARK—BY FOLLYING TH' SOUNDS O' THEM "BLURPS"—ONLY FOLKS WHICH CHAWS "DAID DAWG CHOMPIN' T'BACCY" MAKES THET SOUND—AN' AH HAD JEST STUFFED TH' ONLY WAD OF IT INTO TH' CLOCK !!

BLAST IT !! AH WOULDA HAD ANOTHER BOOTIFUL CORPSE T' MAH CREDIT—EF ONLY AH COULDA RESISTED THET CHOMPIN' T'BACCY !!— BLURP!

Copr. 1942 by United Feature Syndicate, Inc.
Tm. Reg. U. S. Pat. Off.—All rights reserved

AH IS **YOUNG YANCEY** !! 50 Y'ARS AGO, WHEN THIS CLOCK STRUCK 12—MAH BOOTIFUL BRIDE-TO-BE RAN OFF WIF TH' BEST MAN !! SINCE THET HOUR, AH HAS MADE IT MAH CAREER T'KILL **ANY** BOOTIFUL GAL WHO HAPPENS T'BE NEAR THIS CLOCK—AT MIDNIGHT! **WHUT TIME IS IT, SON?**

AH'LL PULL OUT MAH WATCH AN' LOOK—

Copr. 1942 by United Feature Syndicate, Inc.
Tm. Reg. U. S. Pat. Off.—All rights reserved

IT'S 12:03

OUCH !!

YO' SHORE FELL FO' THET ONE !!

HYAW!!—AN' NOW, AH ADDS **ANOTHER** BOOTIFUL CORPSE T'MAH SCORE !!

HALP!

Li'L ABNER

by AL CAPP !!

THE NEXT DAY

SOCIETY LEADER NABBED AS MOONSHINER!!

SOCIETY WAS AGOG TODAY AT THE NEWS THAT MRS. BEATRIX BOPSHIRE HAD BEEN ARRESTED FOR OPERATING AN ILLEGAL WHISKEY STILL IN THE BATH ROOM OF HER PALATIAL MANSION.

AMONG HER GUESTS WAS A MR. YOUNG YANCEY, LON WANTED FOR MURDER IN THE SOUTH, WHO IS BEING SENT BACK TO KENTUCKY. MRS. BOPSHIRE'S NAME WILL DEFINITELY BE OUT OF THE NEXT SOCIAL REGISTER

LI'L ABNER

by AL CAPP !!

AH GOT A TELLYPHONE! IT'S ALL PAID FO'—BUT, (GULP!) AH DON'T KNOW WHO DONE IT!—TH' MAN SAID—"TH' SUBSCRIBER REQUESTED THET HIS **NAME** BE KEPT PRIVATE !!"

AN'—AH (GULP!) D-DON'T KNOW MAH PHONE NUMBER!—TH' MAN SAID—"TH' SUBSCRIBER REQUESTED TH' **NUMBER** BE KEPT P-PRIVATE !!"

TH' GENNULMAN WHO HAD THIS PHONE PUT IN IS TH' **ONLY** GENNULMAN IN TH' WORLD WHO KNOWS MAH NUMBER!

Copr. 1942 by United Feature Syndicate, Inc.
Tm. Reg. U. S. Pat. Off.—All rights reserved

H-HOPE HE CALLS ME UP!

HE'D BE A DAWGONE FOOL EF HE DIDN'T !!

8-20

'BOUT ONCE EV'RY COUPLA MONTHS, AH PERMITS DAISY MAE T'TAKE A LI'L WALK WIF ME! SHE DESARVES TH' PLEASURE, PORE CRITTER!

8-21

YO' KIN START FOLLYIN'. AH'LL TREAT YO' TO A LI'L WALK WIF ME!

MUCH OBLIGED, LI'L ABNER—BUT AH IS ALL TIED UP!

Copr. 1942 by United Feature Syndicate, Inc.
Tm. Reg. U. S. Pat. Off.—All rights reserved

AH GOTTA SET IN WIF THET CONTRAPTION, IN CASE IT CALLS ME!

WISH'T IT WOULD GO OFF!—WORRYIN' 'BOUT IT IS MAKIN' **A OLD WOOMIN** OUTA ME!

LI'L ABNER

by AL CAPP !!

128

LI'L ABNER
by AL CAPP!!

EXACKLY NINE O'CLOCK!—AN' THAR "IT" GOES—IT'S A-GONNA AX ME THET IMPAWTINT QUESTION—AN' (SOB!) AH'LL SAY **Y-YES!**

BONG!

R-RING!

MIGHT'S WELL! YO' HAINT A CHICKEN NO MO'. YO' IS ON TH' SHADY SIDE O' **EIGHTEEN!** AN' THET HAINT GOOD!

Y-YES!! GOO'BYE!— IT'S VOICE SOUNDED KINDA STRAINED—IT SAID A SURPRISE IS A-WAITIN' ME AT TH' DOGPATCH TELEGRAPH OFFICE—

AH'LL GO WIF YO', T'GIVE YO' AWAY—AN' **GOOD RIDDANCE!**

THEY LEAVE——10 MINUTES LATER.

BONG! BONG!

EXACKLY NINE O'CLOCK! THET OLE TIMEPIECE IS **NEVAH** WRONG!

TOWN HALL

AT THE SAME INSTANT!!— BACK AT DAISY MAE'S—

TH' PHONE IS RINGIN'—AN' NOBODY'S HOME. ONLY SOCIABLE THING FO' ME T'DO IS CHAW TH' FAT WIF IT!!

RING!

WILL AH MARRY YO'? **YO' BET!!** WHO IS YO'?—

BE PATIENT! OURS HAS BEEN A STRANGE ROMANCE!

—JUST TO MAKE IT **STRANGER** AND **MORE** ROMANTIC—I WILL MEET YOU AT THE PREACHER'S—WEARING A **MASK!**—YOU WEAR A MASK TOO. AFTER WE'RE MARRIED,—WE'LL UNMASK!!

SHO' NUFF, STRANGER!

HA! HA!— MY SCHEME **WORKED!!** WHEN I REMOVE THE MASK—IT WILL BE TOO LATE—THAT GORGEOUS CREATURE WILL BE **MINE!**

MARRYIN' DAN FUNERALS + MARRIAGES ALSO HAY + FEED

DOGPATCH TELEGRAPH OFFICE

131

LI'L ABNER

by AL CAPP!!

Panel 1:
TWO DOLLAHS—CORRECT!

AN' NOW THET WE IS MARRIED—LE'S UNMASK!

IT'S (CHUCKLE!) TOO LATE TO CHANGE YOUR MIND NOW—BUT I WARN YOU, DARLING—MY FACE IS HORRIBLE!

Panel 2:
WHUT'S SO HORRIBLE ABOUT IT? YO' IS MAH FAVORITE TYPE!

I'VE BEEN TRICKED!!

9-3

Panel 3:
MEANWHILE: AT THE TELEGRAPH OFFICE NEXT DOOR.

YOUR NUMBER WAS DIALED AT RANDOM BY "THE POT O' GOLD-POLISH" PROGRAM. YOU'VE WON THIS CHECK FOR ONE HUNDRED DOLLARS!

A HUNDERD DOLLAHS! OH—HAPPY DAY!!

Panel 4:
BUT, IT CAN BE USED ONLY TO PURCHASE GOLD-POLISH! —ONE HUNDRED DOLLARS' WORTH!

B-BUT, WE HAINT GOT NO GOLD!

SHECKS! WHUT DOES YO' THINK THIS TOOTH IS MADE OF? AH KIN POLISH IT FO' TH' REST O' MAH NATCHERAL LIFE!!

Panel 5:
DUNNO WHUT WE WILL DO WIF THET TELLY-PHONE NOW!!

DON'T WORRY 'BOUT IT!!—WHILE YO' WAS AWAY—THEY COME AN' YANKED IT OUT!!

Panel 6:
THET NOSEY McBLABBER!! HE'S ALLUS STICKIN' HIS NOSE INTO OTHER FOLKSES' BUSINESS! IT'LL BE TH' DEATH O'HIM YET!

LITTLE DOES GRANNY REALIZE THAT HER CASUAL COMMENT WILL BECOME A TRAGIC PROPHECY!!!

9-4

Panel 7:
LI'L ABNER—THEY'S HOLDIN' TH' ANNOOAL RASSLIN' AN' PIE-EATIN' CONTESTS, AT PINEAPPLE JUNCTION, TOMORRY NIGHT! NATCHERLY YO' WILL BE THAR!

RASSLIN' AN' PIES IS M-MAH FAVORITE SPORTS!—BUT (GULP!) AH WILL NOT BE THAR!!

Panel 8:
—ON ACCOUNT OF—TOMORRY NIGHT—AH GOTTA IMPAWTINT INGAGEMENT—WIF A FEMALE OF TH' OPPOSITE SEX!!

(—HM!—CAINT BE DAISY MAE—ON ACCOUNT HE SAID 'T WAS IMPAWTINT. THIS IS NONE O' MAH BUSINESS—SO AH'LL STICK MAH NOSE INTO IT!!—)

LI'L ABNER

by AL CAPP !!

LI'L ABNER by AL CAPP!!

THE PO'K CHOP BENEFIT DANCE.

LI'L ABNER COULDN'T COME— SAID HE HAD A DATE WIF A SARTIN SOMEONE ATOP "DREAMY MOUNTAIN"— W-WOULDN'T TELL ME **WHO**! —SAID HE'D STOP AT **NOTHIN'** T'PREVENT ANYONE **FINDIN'** OUT WHO SHE IS!! THEY IS (SOB!) PROB'LY ATOP "DREAMY MOUNTAIN" N-NOW!!

LOOK!! HYAR COME NOSEY McBLABBER, SCOOTIN' DOWN "DREAMY MOUNT'IN'!"

Copr. 1942 by United Feature Syndicate, Inc.
Tm. Reg. U. S. Pat. Off.—All rights reserved

HALP! HALP!!

NOSEY McBLABBER IS DAID!!

THET ROCK **MURDERED** HIM!!

GRROOANN!

UGH! CAINT MOVE THIS ROCK OFF O' PORE NOSEY, NOHOW!

T-TO MAH D-DYIN' DAY, AH'LL HEAR PORE NOSEY'S SCREAMS— AS HE COME A-TEARIN' DOWN TH' MOUNT'IN, WIF THIS ROCK A-TEARIN' AFTER HIM!!

THET ROCK WERE LIKE SOMETHIN' **HOOMIN** —IT FOLLYED PORE NOSEY FUM TH' TOP O' "DREAMY MOUNT'IN'"—AS EF IT **WANTED** T'KILL HIM!!—

(—"THAR **WERE** SOMETHIN' **HOOMIN** AT TH' TOP O' "DREAMY MOUNT'IN"— NAME OF **LI'L ABNER**! HE HAD A DATE UP THAR – A **SECRET DATE**!")

9-9

Copr. 1942 by United Feature Syndicate, Inc.
Tm. Reg. U. S. Pat. Off.—All rights reserved

AH GOTTA GIT MAH SECRET DATE AWAY FUM HYAR!!

Li'l ABNER

by AL CAPP !!

DOCTOR!! COME A-RUNNIN'! THAR'S BIN A TRAGEDY!

CUSSES!—AH WERE JEST GOIN' OFF FO' A Y'AR'S POST-GRADUATE STUDY AT TH' GOAT AN' MULE HOSPITAL IN KNOXVILLE!

THET TREMENJUS ROCK, ATOP 'DREAMY MOUNT'IN', DONE FELL ON PORE NOSEY McBLABBER! HE'S **UNDER** IT !!—

THET ROCK?—WAL, THEN—HE'S DAID, SHO' NUFF!—NO SENSE ME EVEN LOOKIN' AT HIM!—**AH'LL SIGN TH' DEATH CERTIFICATE**—

9-10

WE COULDN'T MOVE TH' ROCK OFF OF NOSEY, SO WE DECIDED TO LEAVE IT AS HIS TOMBSTONE!

NO, MAMMY, AH **DON'T** WANTA PAY MAH RESPECKS AT NOSEY McBLABBER'S GRAVE!—WHY **SHOULD** AH?

(—"HM—HE'S ACTIN' PEE-KOOLYAR 'BOUT TH' WHOLE THING!—)

(—"HE NEVAH DONE MENSHUNNED TO NOBODY THET **HE** WERE ATOP 'DREAMY MOUNT'IN', THET NIGHT!")

MAY NOSEY McBLABBER REST IN PEACE, 'NEATH THIS ROCK, HE'S A MESS O' GREASE.

"HANGIN' YANCEY"—DISTRICT ATTORNEY OF PINEAPPLE COUNTY—WHICH INCLUDES THE COMMUNITY OF DOGPATCH—

HM—ELECTION TIME'S COMIN' SOON—AN' IT DON'T LOOK GOOD FO' **ME**! ALL AH HAS CONVICTED THIS Y'AR HAS BIN ONE MOONSHINER AN' TWELVE REVENOOERS !!

"WANTED"

9-11

EF ONLY AH COULD **HANG** SOMEONE, MAH POPULARITY WOULD ZOOM UP AGIN! BUT, T' HANG ANYONE—AH'D HAFTA CONVICT HIM OF MURDER !!—

LAST RITES

THE LAST RITES FOR MR. NOSEY McBLABBER WERE HELD YESTERDAY BY HIS SORROWING FELLOW-CITIZENS OF DOGPATCH.

McBLABBER WAS THE VICTIM OF AN ODD ACCIDENT.

A HUGE ROCK CAME HURTLING AFTER HIM FROM THE TOP OF 'DREAMY MOUNTAIN' AND SQUASHED HIM FLATTER THAN A FLOUNDER.

THET COULDN'T HAVE BEEN A MURDER—— UNLESS——— SOMEONE AT THE **TOP**—**PUSHED TH' ROCK!**— SOMEONE WHO **HATED** McBLABBER !!

Li'L ABNER

by AL CAPP !!

IS THAR A HOOMIN BEIN' IN THIS TOWN WHICH WEARS A SIZE 18 SHOE ?

YASSUH, MISTAH "HANGIN' YANCEY!" NAME OF LI'L ABNER YOKUM! **HE** GOT **REAL** FEET !!

HMM!—LEADIN' UP TO—AN' RUNNIN' **AWAY** FUM TH' SPOT WHAR THET HUGE ROCK STARTED ROLLIN' FO' TH' LATE MR. NOSEY McBLABBER—WERE **FOOTPRINTS, SIZE 18** !!

9-12

AH'VE GOT A MURDER CASE !!

A WARRANT FO' TH' ARREST OF LI'L ABNER YOKUM !!

"AHEM!"—TH' FREE AN' INDEPENDENT COMMOONITY O' DOGPATCH, GARDEN SPOT O' TH' MOUNTAINS—NO TAXES, NO ROADS, NO WATER POWER, NO MODERN SANITATION—IN FACT, NO NOTHIN'—ALSO, HAY, GRAIN, AN' FEED, CHEAP AT SOFTHEARTED JOHN'S—-POPOOLAYSHUN TWO HUNDERD—MINUS ONE—O' COURSE, AFTER YO' IS HUNG, EEMEEJUTLY FOLLYIN' YO' FAIR TRIAL——HEREBY CHARGES YO' WIF MURDER! **YO' MURDERER !!**—

SUMMONS

WILL YO' COME QUIETLY?—OR WILL YO' RESISK !!

BASH!

Copr. 1942 by United Feature Syndicate, Inc.
Tm. Reg. U. S. Pat. Off.—All rights reserved

THAR WERE A SARTIN SWEET SOMEONE, UP ON DREAMY MOUNTAIN WIF YO,' THET NIGHT. ALL SHE GOTTA DO IS TESTIFY YO' DIDN'T PUSH TH' ROCK.

SHE'LL (GULP!) **NEVAH** TESTIFY!

CLICK!

9-14

Li'L ABNER

by **AL CAPP!!**

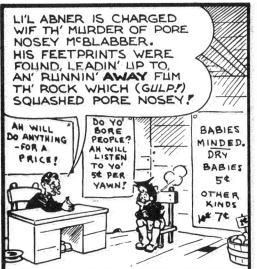

LI'L ABNER

by AL CAPP!!

LI'L ABNER

by AL CAPP !!

AH ARRANGED WIF TH' SHERIFF T'HAVE COUSIN UNBEARABLE JONES PUT IN TH' SAME CELL WIF LI'L ABNER. A FEW HOURS O' THET AN' TH' BOY'LL BE WILLIN' T'DO **ANYTHING** T'GIT RID O' HIM—EVEN TO **TALK**.!!

GREETIN'S, FRIEND !! NO WONDER YO' IS BLUE! WHO WOULDN'T BE—WIF A **ROPE** AWAITIN' FO' HIS NECK !!

CLICK!!

AH'LL TRY T'GIT YO' MIND OFF TH' FACT YO' IS SHORELY GONNA BE **HANGED** (CHUCKLE). WHICH REMINDS ME OF A JOKE—'BOUT A FELLA WHO WAS BEIN' **HANGED**— YO'LL INJOY THIS !

AN' THAR HE WAS—A-CHOKIN' AN' A-GURGLIN'-- **HIS FACE WERE BLUE — HIS EYES WERE A-POPPIN' OUT**---

OH !! YO' IS UNBEARABLE !!

NATCHERLY !!

9-24

Dear Available:

Ah don't want to say nothin' spiteful about yore relatives.

All ah will say is that yore cuzzin Unbearable shore is.

Ah will do anything if yo will take him away. Anything!

yoresin agony

Li'l Abner

HA !! – HE HAS BROKEN DOWN !! – **AT LAST**, HE WILL NAME HIS FAIR COMPANION OF THE NIGHT O' TH' MURDER !!

9-25

AH CAIN'T BEAR YO' NO LONGER, UNBEARABLE !! TH' CELL-DOOR IS WIDE OPEN !! PLEASE EXCAPE!

Z-Z-Z

ON **ONE** CONDISHUN! EF YO' WILL NAME YO' FAIR COMPANION ON TH' NIGHT O' TH' MURDER !!

AWRIGHT! (SOB!) AH'LL TALK! SHE WAS---

LI'L ABNER by AL CAPP!!

TH' CELL-DOOR IS WIDE OPEN !! AH'LL (*SOB*) DO ANYTHING, EF YO'LL ONLY **USE** IT !! AH'LL EVEN TELL YO' WHO AH WAS WIF, TH' NIGHT O' TH' MURDER !! IT WAS---

AH CAIN'T BEAR YO' NO LONGER-- UNBEARABLE !!

COUNTY JAIL

AH LEFT THET CELL-DOOR OPEN A-PURPOSE !!--HOPIN' YO'D EXCAPE !! **GIT OUTA HYAR !!**

LATER:

THANK YO' FO' TRYIN', UNBEARABLE ! YO' WAS MAH LAST HOPE !! **NOTHIN'** KIN MAKE HIM TALK , NOW !-- HE'S SHORE T'HANG !!--

PROCLAMATION!

THE JURY TO TRY THE MURDERER YOKUM ON A CHARGE OF MURDER WILL BE SELECTED IN THE USUAL MANNER, AT THE OLD OAK TREE AT **12** TODAY--

SIGNED
T.J. "HANGIN'" TOLLIVER
JUDGE
B.O. "HANGIN'" YANCEY
DISTRICT ATTORNEY
A.B. "HANGIN'" McSKONK
SHERIFF

12 O'CLOCK

TWELVE GOOD WIMMEN AN' TRUE !

WE HAS ELIMINATED TH' OPPOSIN' SEX--AS WHEN DON'T WE !

(--HM !-- AN ALL-WOOMIN JURY !! ANY IMBECILE WOULD KNOW ENOUGH TO APPEAL TO THAR **GENTLER** SIDE ! AH'LL APPEAL TO THAR GENTLER SIDE !--)

LI'L ABNER by AL CAPP!!

The state versus Li'l Abner Yokum, for the murder of Mr. Nosey McBlabber. The judge is "Hangin'" Tolliver; the district attorney is "Hangin'" Yancey; and the sheriff is "Hangin'" McSkonk.

Ladies o' th' jury—ah hopes t'convince yo'-all thet Mr. Nosey McBlabber was murdered by a certain feend! TAKE TH' STAND, FEEND!!!

GULP! Y-YASSUH!

(—"PSST! Remember whut ah told yo'! We gotta try to sway this all-woomin jury!")

MY!—Whut a fine figger!!

So attractive!

Sharp, haint he?

(—"This is vurry hoo-miliatin'! —Ah hopes it's legal!")

Yo' admits yo' had a date wif a "Sartin sweet someone," th' night McBlabber was murdered!—Yo' admits yo' said yo'd stop at nothin' t' prevent anyone fum findin' out who thet "Sartin sweet someone" was!!

RIGHT!

RIGHT!

Yo' admits yo' an' thet "Sartin sweet someone" was up on "Dreamy Mount'in," while McBlabber was thar!—Yo' admits it was YO' footprints leadin' up t'th' rock thet killed McBlabber!—Yo' admits YO' killed McBlabber!

RIGHT! RIGHT!

RIGHT! RIGHT!

NO!

Th' only way yo' kin prove yo' DIDN'T do it is by producin' th' only witness who kin testify yo' didn't— "THET SARTIN SWEET SOMEONE!"

Ah'll NEVAH ax her t'testify! Ah'll nevah HOOMILIATE her by revealin' who she is!! NEVAH!!

AH CAIN'T STAND IT NO LONGER! AH IS THET SARTIN SWEET SOMEONE!

LI'L ABNER

by AL CAPP !!

Li'l ABNER by AL CAPP!!

146

LI'L ABNER by AL CAPP!!

H-HERE'S Y-YOUR DINNER!---

10-8

Copr. 1942 by United Feature Syndicate, Inc.
Tm. Reg. U. S. Pat. Off.—All rights reserved

AN' **NOW** – ON T' DOGPATCH – T' SEE MAH COUSIN – **AVAILABLE JONES!!**

LIFE'S JUST ONE STUPID ROMANCE **AFTER ANOTHER!** –I'VE BEEN ENGAGED **FIVE TIMES** –

10-9

Copr. 1942 by United Feature Syndicate, Inc.
Tm. Reg. U. S. Pat. Off.—All rights reserved

–ALWAYS HOPING THAT THE **NEXT** ONE WOULD BE MY DREAM MAN – BUT – (SIGH!) – EACH ONE WAS DULLER THAN THE LAST!! AT TWENTY-TWO **I'M BORED WITH LOVE!!** –

DOGPATCH! – HAVEN'T BEEN HERE SINCE I WAS A CHILD! HM! – I SEEM TO REMEMBER AN OLD CHARACTER WHO USED TO HAUNT A CAVE HEREABOUTS ---

"OLD MAN MOSE," THE LOCAL YOKELS CALLED HIM – AND THEY REALLY BELIEVED **HE COULD FORETELL THE FUTURE!** TEE HEE!! IT MIGHT BE FUN TO HAVE MINE TOLD–

147

Li'L ABNER
by AL CAPP !!

LI'L ABNER by AL CAPP!!

MAH PROPHECY T'YO', YO' HEART-BREAKIN' LI'L VARMINT, IS AS FOLLOWS ———

"WHEN YO' HAS FOUND YO' *SEVENTH* SWAIN, YO'LL LONG T'SHARE LIFE WITH 'IM! HIDE YO' CHARMS, USE YO' BRAIN— *BUT BEWARE O' MOUNT'IN RHYTHM!*"

B-BUT WHAT DOES IT MEAN?

FIGGER IT OUT FO' YO'SELF!! AH HAS SPOKEN!!

OL' MAN MOSE KEEP OUT!!

—?—?—WHEN I'VE FOUND MY *SEVENTH* SWAIN—?—?— B-BUT I'VE ONLY BEEN ENGAGED TO *FIVE* BOYS! OH, WELL—I'LL FIND A SIXTH—PERMIT HIM TO FALL MADLY IN LOVE WITH ME—BRUSH HIM OFF, PRONTO—

Copr. 1942 by United Feature Syndicate, Inc.
Tm. Reg. U. S. Pat. Off.—All rights reserved

—AND THEN (*SIGH!*)— NUMBER *SEVEN* WILL COME ALONG!!—AND —I'LL—LONG—TO—SHARE —MY LIFE———WITH—HIM—!!

10-13

TH' SUN IS SHININ'—TH' CATFISH IS BITIN'—MAH STUMMICK IS A-BUSTIN' WIF PO'KCHOPS! OH, HAPPY, HAPPY LIFE!!

SADIE HAWKINS DAY NOV. 7

10-14

WISHT AH WAS DAID!!

YO' WANTS ME T'PROPHESY WHUT'S GONNA HAPPEN T'YO', COME SADIE HAWKINS DAY? STEP CLOSER, SON—AH DON'T WANT YO' T'TOPPLE OVER TH' EDGE, WHEN AH PRO-NOUNCES YO' DOOM!

AH HAINT SO DOOM! AH IS MERELY NINETEEN AN' IS IN TH' SIXTH GRADE!

Copr. 1942 by United Feature Syndicate, Inc.
Tm. Reg. U. S. Pat. Off.—All rights reserved

LI'L ABNER

by **AL CAPP!!**

G-GO AHEAD, OLE MAN MOSE! T-TELL ME WHUT'S GONNA HAPPEN T'ME, C-COME SADIE HAWKINS D-DAY. AH'LL BE B-BRAVE 'BOUT IT----

MAH PROPHECY IS AS FOLLOWS-

"TH' END WILL COME—AN' YO' MUST FACE IT!!"

AH M-MUST F-FACE IT, HUH?—

RIGHT!! AH HAS SPOKEN! GOO'BYE!!

OL' MAN MOSE KEEP OUT!

10-15

(-"AH MUST F-FACE IT —SOB!"—)

ARE YOU FACING THE RIGHT WAY, SON?—

OLE MAN MOSE SAID THET ON THIS "SADIE HAWKINS DAY"—TH' END WILL COME—AN' HE IS (GULP!) NEVAH WRONG!

10-16

WHAT IS "SADIE HAWKINS DAY"?—WHY DOES IT INSPIRE SUCH TERROR IN OUR HERO?—FOR THOSE UNFAMILIAR WITH THE FACTS, WE REPRINT THE FOLLOWING HISTORICAL DATA-

SADIE HAWKINS WAS THE DAUGHTER OF ONE OF THE EARLIEST SETTLERS OF DOGPATCH, HEKZEBIAH HAWKINS. SHE WAS THE HOMELIEST GAL IN ALL THEM HILLS.

PAPPY!-AH IS TWENTY Y'ARS OLE TODAY!-EV'RY OTHER GAL IN DOGPATCH MAH AGE IS MARRIED UP. HOW COME AH HAIN'T?

HAVE PATIENCE, DOTTER!-YO'LL PROB'LY BE GITTIN' A OFFER ANY DAY NOW.

FIFTEEN YEARS LATER~

PAPPY!-AH HAIN'T GOT A OFFER YET!-YO' GOTTA GIT ME A HUSBAND OR YO'LL HAVE ME ON YO' HANDS FO' TH' REST O' YO' NATCHERAL LIFE!!-

DOTTER!-THET SHO' WOULD BE AWFUL!-AH'LL GIT YO' A HUSBAND T'MORRY!-AH GOT A PLAN!!

LI'L ABNER by AL CAPP!!

"SADIE HAWKINS DAY"—

FOR 15 YEARS SADIE HAWKINS, HOMELY DAUGHTER OF DOGPATCH'S EARLIEST SETTLER, HAD FAILED TO CATCH A HUSBAND—

HER PAPPY, IN DESPERATION ONE DAY, CALLED TOGETHER ALL THE ELIGIBLE BACHELORS OF DOGPATCH.

BOYS!!—SINCE NONE O' YO' HAS BEEN MAN ENOUGH T' MARRY MAH DOTTER—AH GOTTA TAKE FIRM MEASURES!!

GULP! GULP! GULP!

10-17

AH DECLARES T'DAY "SADIE HAWKINS DAY"—WHEN AH FIRES—ALL O' YO' KIN START A-RUNNIN'!—WHEN AH FIRES AGIN—AFTER GIVIN' YO' A FAIR START—SADIE STARTS A-RUNNIN'. TH' ONE SHE KETCHES'LL BE HER HUSBAND!—LE'S GO!!

BOOM

WELL, SADIE DID CATCH ONE OF THE BOYS. THE OTHER SPINSTERS OF DOGPATCH RECKONED IT WERE SUCH A GOOD IDEA THAT SADIE HAWKINS DAY WAS MADE AN ANNUAL AFFAIR.

LI'L ABNER!! HAINT YO' GONNA PRACTICE RUNNIN' FO' SADIE HAWKINS DAY, NOVEMBER 7TH?—

WHUT'S TH' USE!!—OLE MAN MOSE DONE PROPHESIED TH' END WILL COME!! AH IS (SOB!) A GONER!!

INSTEAD O' GOIN' CATFISHIN', DEAR, WILL YO' GIVE TH' BABIES THAR BOTTLES, DEAR?

YES, DEAR!

SALOMEY'S SNORIN' DISTURBS TH' BABIES, DEAR. SO, WILL YO' PLEASE LOCK SALOMEY OUT FO' TH' NIGHT, DEAR?

LOCK SALOMEY OUT FO' TH' NIGHT? (SOB!) YES, DEAR!!

10-19

AN' NOW, DEAR, YO' WILL COMMENCE A-KISSIN' ME—WHICH WILL GO ON FO' SEVERAL HOURS AS USUAL, EV'RY EVENIN', DEAR—

A-KISSIN' YO' FO' SEV'RAL HOURS AS USUAL—EV'RY (SOB!) EVENIN'? Y-YES, DEAR!!

AH GOTTA STOP EE-MAGININ' THINGS!!—OH, IT'S INHOOMIN—BUT AH GOTTA FACE IT!! OLE MAN MOSE SAID SO—AN' (SOB!)—MOSE KNOWS!!——

Li'l Abner by Al Capp!!

Panel 1: I'M **SO** GLAD YOU DECIDED TO COME, DEAR! — I'M OPENING THE LODGE WITH A COSTUME PARTY TONIGHT!! / BUT MOTHER — I DIDN'T BRING A COSTUME!

Panel 2: I'VE A DELICIOUS IDEA! — THE DRESSES YOU WORE WHEN YOU LIVED HERE AS A CHILD ARE IN THE ATTIC. YOU'RE **STILL** ABOUT THE SAME SIZE! OH, YOU'LL LOOK **CAPTIVATING**!! / BUT — DEFINITELY! (—"I'M OUT TO CAPTIVATE NUMBER SIX!"—

Copr. 1942 by United Feature Syndicate, Inc.
Tm. Reg. U. S. Pat. Off.—All rights reserved

10-20

Panel 3: — AND THEN BRUSH HIM OFF — BECAUSE — "WHEN I HAVE FOUND MY **SEVENTH** SWAIN — I'LL LONG TO SHARE LIFE WITH HIM — I MUST HIDE MY CHARMS — USE MY BRAIN BUT — **BEWARE OF MOUNTAIN RHYTHM**!!"

Panel 4: —?—?— I UNDERSTAND IT ALL — EXCEPT — **THE LAST LINE**!!

Panel 5: OH, TINY! — YOU LOOK LIKE AN INNOCENT CHILD — STEPPING OUT INTO THE WORLD WITH SHY, TRUSTING EYES! / UHUH! — (—"ACCORDING TO OLD MAN MOSE — AND THAT OLD FOSSIL **KNOWS** — AS SOON AS MY 6TH ROMANCE IS OVER —)

Panel 6: (—"MY **REAL** ROMANCE WILL COME ALONG! — SO I WANT TO GET THE 6TH OVER WITH — **PRONTO! ANYONE** WILL DO — EVEN **HIM**!!"—) / (—"A CUTE KID — BUT WHAT IS **SHE** DOING UP SO LATE?")

10-21

Panel 7: A LIGHT? — YES, OF COURSE — BUT — — — — ?—?— ARE YOU ALLOWED TO SMOKE? / WHERE THERE'S HEAT — THERE'S ALWAYS SMOKE!!

Panel 8: THAT L-LOOK SHE GAVE ME!! IT'S G-GOT ME ALL C-CONFUSED!!

Copr. 1942 by United Feature Syndicate, Inc.
Tm. Reg. U. S. Pat. Off.—All rights reserved

152

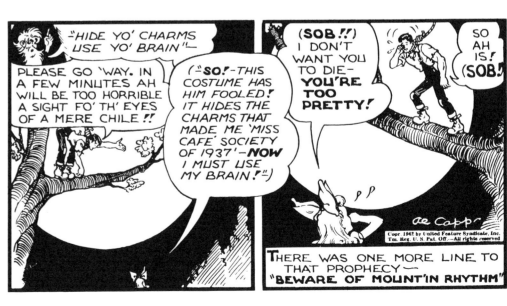

155

156

LI'L ABNER

by AL CAPP!!

(SIGH!!)—ALL OTHER HANDSOME BACHELORS HEAP WORRIED, ON ACCOUNT SQUAWS GONNA CHASE UM, COME SADIE HAWKINS DAY. WISH LONESOME POLECAT WAS WORRIED. WISH SOME SQUAW WOULD CHASE ME!!

Copr. 1942 by United Feature Syndicate, Inc.
Tm. Reg. U. S. Pat. Off.—All rights reserved

—EVERY SADIE HAWKINS DAY LONESOME POLECAT, HE RUN VERY SLOW—IMITATING MATING CRIES OF WATER BUFFALO—BUT NO FEMALE NEVER CHASE ME—EXCEPT ONE—

—AN' THAT WAS FEMALE PANTHER! (SIGH!) SHE ONLY WANT TO EAT ME! WISH I COULD MEET NICE, PLUMP, 100% AMERICAN GIRL!!

ME 100% PLUMP AMERICAN GIRL!

11-3

THEY CALL ME PRINCESS "I-NEVER-FIGHT-BACK!"

THAT SO NICE TO KNOW!

WHUFFO' IS YO' SO EXCITED, LONESOME POLECAT, OLE PAL!?

OH, MY HAIRLESS FRIEND, JOE!—A BEAUTIFUL SQUAW, SHE GONNA CHASE ME, IN SADIE HAWKINS DAY RACE, NOVEMBER 7TH!

KICKAPOO JOY JUICE

DON'T WORRY! AH'LL SAVE YO', OLE PAL!! AH'LL BASH HER HAID IN!

I SINK TOMMYHAWK IN YO' SKULL, IF YO' DO, OLE PAL!! WE FULL OF LOVE FOR EACH OTHER, AN', AFTER SHE CATCH ME, WE WILL SETTLE DOWN IN ROSE-COVERED WIGWAM!!

11-4
Copr. 1942 by United Feature Syndicate, Inc.
Tm. Reg. U. S. Pat. Off.—All rights reserved

YO' MEANS—YO' IS GONNA MOVE OUTA OUR BACHELOR APARTMENT, OLE PAL?

YOU SAID IT, OLE PAL!!

AFTER ALL THESE Y'ARS—LOVE BREAKS US UP!!

(SOB!) AH HATES LOVE!!—

159

Li'L ABNER by AL CAPP !!

THE SADIE HAWKINS DAY RACE IS ON !!!

OH, (SOB !!) **PLEASE** DON'T KETCH HIM !—D-DON'T BREAK UP OUR HAPPY HOME !!—

I HAVE CAPTURED YOU, BRAVE WARRIOR!

IS **GOOD!**

HE ALLUS GITS A GOOD START ON ME—BUT AH'LL CLOSE IN, PURTY SOON !!

(*CHUCKLE!*) ALL AH **NEEDS** IS A GOOD START! AH GOT A HIDIN' PLACE **NOBODY** KNOWS 'BOUT —'CEPT ME—AN' THET INNER-CENT CHILE!

S-SHE'S GONNA KETCH ME—BUT AH **CAIN'T** PASS **THET SPOT!!** WHUT'S THAR—IS **UNMENTIONABLE!**

11-10 Copr. 1942 by United Feature Syndicate, Inc. Tm. Reg. U. S. Pat. Off.—All rights reserved

(SOB !!)—YO' **GOT HIM**—AN' HE'S TH' LAST O' TH' SEEGARSTOR INJUNS !!

YOU LAST OF SEEGARSTOR INDIANS ?

IS TRUE!

ME LAST OF **MOHICANS!** SEEGARSTORS AN' MOHICANS, **BLOOD ENEMIES!**—I NOT WANT TO TAKE ALL OF YOU—JUST **SCALP!!**

SWISH!

OUCH!

SCALPED-CLEAN AS A WHISTLE! —BUT SHE'S LEAVIN' TH' REST O' HIM FO' **ME!** OUR HAPPY HOME HAIN'T BROKEN UP!

(*CHUCKLE!*)—SHE SAID SHE WAS GONNA KETCH ME WIF A **"SECRET WEAPON"** —BUT—SO FAR'S AH KIN SEE—SHE HAINT **GOT** NO SECRET WEAPON !! TSK !!—WISH'T AH C'D RUN AS FAST AS THET HAN'SOME DAWG !!

11-11

THANKS FO' KETCHIN' HIM FO' ME, **"SECRET WEAPON !!"**

AH SEEN HIM DIVE INTO THET HOLLOW TRUNK!

OOH!

A FEW MINUTES LATER—THE FINISH LINE !!

STOP A-CHEWIN' HIS LAIG OFF, "SECRET WEAPON," OR AH WON'T HAVE 'NUFF LEFT T' MARRY UP WIF !!

MARRY ME UP T' TH' CONTENTS O' THIS HOLLER TRUNK, SAM!

A **DOUBLE WEDDIN'!** —HOW ROMANTICAL!

Copr. 1942 by United Feature Syndicate, Inc. Tm. Reg. U. S. Pat. Off.—All rights reserved

AN' NOW—YO' IS ALL-**MEN** AN' **WIFES!**

COME OUTA TH' TRUNK, HONEY! YO' IS **MINE!** —ALL MINE !!

GRRR !!

HALP !!

LI'L ABNER

by AL CAPP !!

Li'l ABNER

by AL CAPP !!

Li'l ABNER by AL CAPP!!

NOW—**AH DIVES INTO MAH SECRET HIDIN'-PLACE!**—OH, BLESS THET SWEET INNOCENT LI'L CHILE— SHE DONE **SAVED** ME!

(—"I'VE SAVED HIM—FOR **MYSELF!!**")

11.
Copr. 1942 by United Feature Syndicate, Inc.
Tm. Reg. U. S. Pat. Off.—All rights reserved

NOW—TO GO BACK AND START FROM THE STARTING LINE **!!**—I BROUGHT MY BIRTH CERTIFICATE TO PROVE THAT I WAS BORN IN DOGPATCH, **OVER 22 YEARS AGO**— AND AM PERFECTLY ELIGIBLE **!!**

BACK AT THE STARTING LINE!

AT L-LAST AH IS FREE O' UNMENTIONABLE JONES-BUT-OH, LI'L ABNER, WHAR **IS** YO'?

HM!—YO' **IS** ELIGIBLE, SHO' NUFF!—GO AHAID!!—

OLE MAN MOSE PROPHESIED—"TH' END WILL COME, AN' YO' MUS' **FACE** IT!"— WAL (CHUCKLE!) THET'S ONE PROPHECY, THET **WONT** COME TRUE**!!**

—"WHEN YO' HAS FOUND YO' 7TH SWAIN, YO'LL LONG T'SHARE LIFE WIF HIM— HIDE YO' CHARMS, USE YO' BRAIN— BUT— BEWARE O' MOUNT'IN RHYTHM!"

Copr. 1942 by United Feature Syndicate, Inc.
Tm. Reg. U. S. Pat. Off.—All rights reserved

OH— WHAR'S LI'L ABNER??

(—"I'VE DONE EVERY-THING THE PROPHECY TOLD ME TO— AND IT'S ALL WORKING OUT BEAUTIFULLY!—HE'S **IN** THERE!")

11-18

(—"WISH I COULD FIGURE OUT THAT LAST LINE! OH, WELL—IT DOESN'T MATTER—I'VE GOT HIM NOW!!")

(—"HM!—WONDER WHUFFO THET CUTE LI'L GAL IS MESSIN' 'ROUN' THET TREE!!")

166

LI'L ABNER by AL CAPP!!

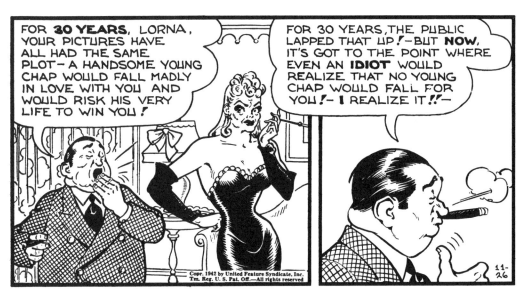

For **30 years**, Lorna, your pictures have all had the same plot — a handsome young chap would fall madly in love with you and would risk his very life to win you!

For 30 years, the public lapped that up!—But **now**, it's got to the point where even an **idiot** would realize that no young chap would fall for you!—I realize it!!—

Is that so!!—Well, let me assure you that there are **thousands** of handsome young chaps who'd **gladly** fall madly in love with me!!

Name one!

I can't.

That's what I thought!! You're **through**, Lorna Goon, unless ---unless--- him--- **Great Scott!**—d-do I dare ??—

Prison Gates Open For T.T. Wolfnagel.

T.T. Wolfnagel, world's greatest publicity man, whose last and most sensational stunt earned him the plaudits of millions, and a ten-year stretch at the state penitentiary, will be released today, after having served his full sentence.

O'Droolihan!! It was fine of you to remember me!! Last time I saw you, ten years ago, you were managing that broken-down glamour girl, Lorna Goon. She's died of old age, I suppose!!

No such luck! I'm **still** managing her—and she **still** thinks she's a glamour girl!!—

Old pal, can you figure out a publicity stunt that'll make that hunk of early Americana a sensation again?

Hm-m!—For 10 years in there I spent my evenings working out a masterpiece— **the greatest, most dangerous publicity stunt of all time!!—**

It'll make a sensation out of **anyone** — but it'll undoubtedly send **me** to the chair! Still—I couldn't **live** with myself, if I didn't try it!! **Let's go!!**—

LI'L ABNER by AL CAPP !!

IT TOOK ME **TEN YEARS** TO WORK IT OUT—THE **GREATEST, MOST DANGEROUS PUBLICITY STUNT OF ALL TIME.!!**—THEY'LL GIVE ME THE HOT SEAT FOR **THIS** ONE—BUT IT'S TOO GREAT **NOT** TO PULL!!

CAN YOU GIVE ME AN IDEA, WOLF-NAGEL?

ON CHRISTMAS EVE, THE PRESIDENT WILL GIVE HIS USUAL CHRISTMAS GREETINGS TO THE NATION. EVERY MAN, WOMAN AND CHILD IN AMERICA WILL BE LISTENING IN—**IT'LL BE THE GREATEST AUDIENCE ON EARTH!!**

AND—JUST BEFORE THE PRESIDENT SPEAKS—THIS GREAT AUDIENCE WILL HEAR A HANDSOME YOUNG CHAP **ACTUALLY KILL HIMSELF**—WHILE CRYING OUT HIS HOPELESS LOVE FOR **LORNA GOON!!**

IT'S **STUPENDOUS!!** BUT WHERE COULD YOU FIND SUCH A CHAP!?

Copr. 1942 by United Feature Syndicate, Inc.
Tm. Reg. U.S. Pat. Off.—All rights reserved
11-28

I'VE FOUND HIM!

WINS BLUSHING CONTEST

LI'L ABNER YO

WINS BLUSHIN CONTEST

YOU CAN GET THIS BOY TO **KILL HIMSELF**, WHILE CRYING OUT HIS HOPELESS LOVE FOR THAT OLD WRECK, LORNA GOON, ON A NATIONAL HOOK-UP, JUST BEFORE THE PRESIDENT SPEAKS, **ON CHRISTMAS EVE??**

I HAVE IT ALL WORKED OUT!

IF YOU CAN **DO** IT—LORNA GOON WILL BE THE MOST **TALKED-ABOUT** STAR IN THE WORLD!—PRODUCERS WILL FIGHT FOR HER SERVICES!!

I CAN DO IT!

OF COURSE, IT'S KINDA TOUGH ON THE BOY—**BUT WHY SHOULD HE STAND IN THE WAY OF LORNA GOON'S CAREER!?**

I'LL GET TO WORK ON IT, IMMEDIATELY!

Copr. 1942 by United Feature Syndicate, Inc.
Tm. Reg. U.S. Pat. Off.—All rights reserved
11-30

169

IN ORDER TO GET THIS YOKUM LAD IN THE PROPER FRAME OF MIND **TO KILL HIMSELF ON CHRISTMAS EVE** FOR THE LOVE OF LORNA GOON — HE MUST **NOT** SEE HER! HE MUST SEE **ONLY** A **PHOTOGRAPH** OF HER — RETOUCHED BY "SMASH-UP" SMITH!!

"SMASH-UP" SMITH? — WASN'T HE THE GENIUS WHO PAINTED THAT FAMOUS HIGHWAY BILLBOARD? IT WAS A GIRL'S FACE — **LOOKING RIGHT AT YOU** —

THOSE **EYES**!! THEY WERE SO FASCINATING — SO **IRRESISTIBLE** — THAT, ON THE FIRST DAY THE BILLBOARD APPEARED, **20,000** CARS WERE SMASHED UP!!

RIGHT! THE DRIVERS WERE HELD **SPELLBOUND** BY THAT **LOOK**!!

— AND, AS I REMEMBER, "SMASH-UP" SMITH WAS FORBIDDEN BY LAW — EVER TO PAINT AGAIN!!

HE IS THE MAN WHO MUST RETOUCH THE PHOTOGRAPH OF LORNA GOON — AND THAT IS ONLY **PART** OF MY PLAN!!

12-1

Copr. 1942 by United Feature Syndicate, Inc.
Tm. Reg. U. S. Pat. Off. — All rights reserved

B-BUT — THE JUDGE WARNED ME — THAT — IF I EVER PAINTED AGAIN — IT WOULD MEAN — A **LIFE TERM**!!

"SMASH-UP!" THIS IS TO BE THE GREATEST PUBLICITY STUNT OF THE **AGES**!! YOUR ARTISTIC SOUL WON'T **LET** YOU REFUSE!!

YOU'RE **RIGHT,** BLAST YOU!! — I C-CAN'T REFUSE! WHAT IF THEY DO SEND ME UP FOR LIFE!! — **MY NAME WILL GO DOWN IN HISTORY!!**

YOU'RE A **TRUE** ARTIST, "SMASH-UP."

12-2

THE YOKUM LAD MUST NEVER SEE LORNA GOON HERSELF — HE MUST SEE **ONLY** THIS PHOTOGRAPH OF HER — **RETOUCHED**, IN YOUR OWN DEVASTATING WAY!!

UGH!! WHAT A MAP!! RETOUCHING **THAT** WILL TAKE EVERY OUNCE OF MY **GENIUS**!!

Copr. 1942 by United Feature Syndicate, Inc.
Tm. Reg. U. S. Pat. Off. — All rights reserved

THE NEXT DAY —

FINISHED!! THOSE **EYES**! THEY FASCINATE EVEN **ME**!!! —

Li'L ABNER

by AL CAPP!!

HERE'S THE RETOUCHED PHOTO-GRAPH, WOLFNAGEL! I WARN YOU NOT TO LOOK AT IT, WITHOUT WEARING SMOKED GLASSES! THOSE *EYES*—THEY'RE MY MASTERPIECE *!!* THEY'RE *IRRESISTIBLE.!!*

THANKS, SMASH-UP!—AND NOW FOR THE FINISHING TOUCH—THAT ONLY *MELVIN SMELVIN* CAN GIVE IT!

(—*"TWENTY YEARS AGO*, THE OWNER OF THE PALACE THEATRE ORDERED SMELVIN TO CREATE A PLEASANT SPRAY FOR THE THEATRE —*TO ATTRACT PATRONS!"*)

(—*"THE SPRAY WAS SO IRRESISTIBLE*, THE AUDIENCE REFUSED TO *LEAVE !!* COURT ORDERS, TEAR BOMBS, THE STATE MILITIA— *NOTHING* WOULD MAKE 'EM BUDGE — *SO* BEWITCHED WERE THEY BY *THAT SPRAY!!* —THEY FINALLY HAD TO BURN THE THEATRE DOWN, TO GET 'EM OUT *!!*)

12-3

(—*"SMELVIN WAS ORDERED BY THE COURTS NEVER* TO CREATE ANOTHER PERFUME. BUT, HE *MUST* CREATE *ONE* MORE *!!*— THE ESSENCE OF *FRIED PO'K CHOP*, TO SPRAY OVER THIS PHOTOGRAPH *!!*—")

YOU WANT ME TO CREATE THE *IRRESISTIBLE AROMA OF FRIED PO'K CHOP*, TO SPRAY ON A PHOTOGRAPH—? THE JOB *TEMPTS* ME—BUT, I'VE GIVEN UP THE PERFUME BUSINESS—AS YOU CAN PLAINLY SEE!

I'M *SURE* YOU'LL RE-CONSIDER, SMELVIN, WHEN YOU HEAR MY IDEA—PSST! PSST!

WHAT A PUBLICITY STUNT *!!* —TO GET A BOY TO *KILL HIMSELF* FOR THE LOVE OF A *GIRL'S* PHOTOGRAPH —ON CHRISTMAS EVE— OVER A NATIONAL HOOK-UP —JUST BEFORE THE PRESIDENT SPEAKS *!!*

12-4

IT'LL BE THE **GREATEST PUBLICITY STUNT OF ALL TIME!** YOU *CAN'T* REFUSE TO HELP!

NO, WOLFNAGEL —*I CAN'T!* I'LL GET TO WORK ON IT, *IMMEDIATELY!!*

THE NEXT DAY!

THAT IRRESISTIBLE LOOK IN THE EYES —AND THIS IRRESISTIBLE AROMA OF HIS GREATEST WEAKNESS— FRIED PO'K CHOP —*HA!* THIS PHOTO WILL **ENSLAVE HIM !!**

172

Li'L ABNER by AL CAPP!!

WE BIN AWAY OVERNIGHT. TH' CHILE HAS BIN ALONE SINCE YESTIDDY MAWNIN'!!

THAR HE IS!! STARIN' AT A PITCHER — WIF A EX-PRESHUN LIKE A LOVESICK MULE!!

SON! YO' BED HAINT BIN SLEPT IN!!

WHUT YO' BIN DOIN', SINCE WE LEFT YO', SON — 24 HOURS AGO?

NOTHIN' — 'CEPT J-JEST STANDIN' HYAR.

WANTA EAT, SON?

NO!

WANTA SLEEP, SON?

NO!

AH JEST WANTS T' BE ALONE — WIF HER!!

(CHUCKLE!) HE GOT LOVE, PAPPY!

(CHUCKLE!) HE GOT IT BAD! DIDN'T SEE TH' PITCHER — BUT, NATCHERLY, IT'S DAISY MAE!!

AH WANTED HIM T' CARRY THET GENOOWINE, IMMYTAYSHUN, STEEL-FRAMED PHOTY-GRAFT O' ME NEXT T' HIS HEART — BUT (SOB!) — HE DONE THREW IT AWAY! AH S-SEEN HIM DO IT!!

(-"THET STEEL FRAME — IT'S MINE!! AN'— HE'S A-STARIN' AT TH' PITCHER, WIF A STOOPID LOOK! — SO NATCHERLY, HE'S IN LOVE!!-")

SIGH! SIGH! SNIFF! SNIFF! AH-H!

DAISY MAE! — WHUT IS IT, WHEN YO' CAIN'T TAKE YO' EYES OFF'N A GAL'S PITCHER — WHEN YO' CAIN'T EAT, NOR SLEEP, NOR EAT — BUT J-JEST LOOK AT IT...

IT'S LOVE, LI'L ABNER, THASS WHUT IT IS!

THANK YO'! — THET'S WHUT AH THOUGHT IT WAS! — HYAR'S YO' PITCHER, DAISY MAE. IT'S KINDA CRUMPLED, FUM BEIN' IN MAH BACK POCKET. THANKS FO' TH' FRAME.

SNIFF! SNIFF! — AH-H!

Li'l ABNER

by AL CAPP!!

THE HOME OF LORNA GOON, IN HOLLYWOOD

THE MORE I LOOK AT YOU, LORNA, THE LESS I BELIEVE THAT YOU CAN GET **ANY** YOUNG FELLA—WITH THE INTELLIGENCE OF EVEN A FLEA—TO **KILL HIMSELF**, BECAUSE OF HIS HOPELESS LOVE FOR **YOU**!!

HA!

HE WILL KILL HIMSELF BECAUSE OF HIS HOPELESS LOVE FOR HER **PHOTOGRAPH**, O'DROOLIHAN!!—HE WILL NEVER SEE LORNA GOON **HERSELF**!! I ASSURE YOU, THAT ON CHRISTMAS EVE THIS STUNT—**THE GREATEST PUBLICITY STUNT OF ALL TIME, WILL DEFINITELY COME OFF**!!

AND, NOW—**TO DOGPATCH**!! YOUNG YOKUM HAS HAD THE PHOTOGRAPH FOR A WEEK NOW—WHICH MEANS THAT HE IS ALREADY **HOPELESSLY UNDER IT'S FATAL SPELL**!! FROM NOW ON, IT IS MERELY A MATTER OF EGGING HIM ON!!

I'M LOOKING FOR A LAD WITH A STUPID, DAZED EXPRESSION!

DOGPATCH

YO' MUS' MEAN LI'L ABNER, THAR—**HE'S** TH' ONLY ONE ROUN' HYAR WIF A STUPID, DAZED EXPRESSION!

SNIFF! SNIFF! AHHH!

MY BOY, IT'S NONE OF MY BUSINESS—BUT, JUDGING FROM YOUR EXPRESSION, **YOU'RE IN LOVE!** WHO IS THE LUCKY GIRL?

IT HAIN'T A GAL—IT'S MERELY A **PHOTY-GRAFT!** SIGH!

SNIFF! SNIFF! —AH-H!

THIS PHOTY-GRAFT MAKES ME FEEL TH' SAME AS A PAN O' SIZZLIN' PO'K CHOPS—(SIGH!)—**ROMANTICAL**—

OH!—IT'S **SO** NICE T'BE IN LOVE OF A **PHOTY-GRAFT**!!—YO' DON'T HAFTA LISSEN TO THEIR SILLY TALK—YO' DON'T HAFTA GO DANCIN' WIF 'EM!—BEIN' IN LOVE OF A PHOTY-GRAFT GOT **SO** MANY MORE ADVANTAGES THAN BEIN' IN LOVE OF A **REAL** GAL!

BUT, MY BOY—THAT **IS** A PHOTOGRAPH OF A **REAL** GIRL!!

AND—IF YOU LOVE HER PHOTOGRAPH YOU CERTAINLY MUST LOVE **HER**!—DIDN'T YOU REALIZE THAT, **BEFORE**!?

N-NO, SUH—AH **DIDN'T**!! (GULP!) **AH'M A GONER!**

Li'l ABNER

by AL CAPP!!

LI'L ABNER

by AL CAPP!!

AH IS TH' LUCKIEST BOY ALIVE, T'GIT TH' LOVE-ADVICE OF YO', WILLIAM SHAKESPEARE!!

CALL ME BILL! GO AHEAD! POUR YOUR HEART OUT TO HER!!

Deer Lorna Goon:
All mah life, ah has preferred cat-fishin', skonk-huntin' an' rasslin' "Earth-Quake" McGoon to the company of wimmen of the opposite sex.
After seein' yore pitcher ah reelize whut a fool ah has bin!
Ah prefers yore company to thet of cat-fishes, skonks and thet sloppy beast McGoon.

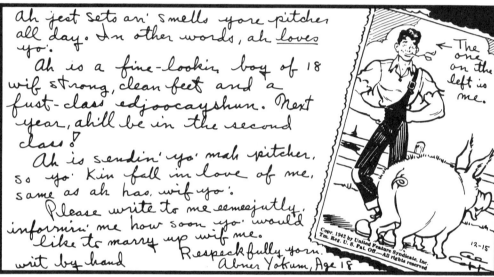

← The one on the left is me.

Ah jest sets an' smells yore pitcher all day. In other words, ah loves yo'.
Ah is a fine-lookin' boy of 18 wif strong, clean feet and a fust-class edjoocayshun. Next year, ah'll be in the second class!
Ah is sendin' yo' mah pitcher, so yo' kin fall in love of me, same as ah has wif yo'.
Please write to me eemeejutly, informin' me how soon yo' would like to marry up wif me.
wr   Respeckfully yorn,
writ by hand   Abner Yokum, Age 18

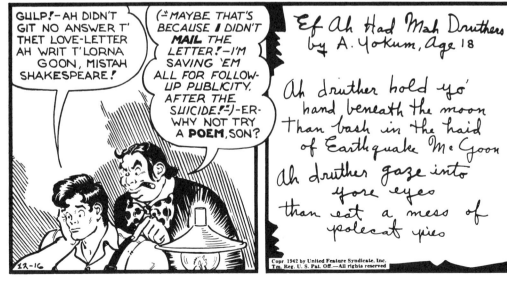

GULP!—AH DIDN'T GIT NO ANSWER T' THET LOVE-LETTER AH WRIT T' LORNA GOON, MISTAH SHAKESPEARE!

(=MAYBE THAT'S BECAUSE I DIDN'T MAIL THE LETTER!—I'M SAVING 'EM ALL FOR FOLLOW-UP PUBLICITY, AFTER THE SUICIDE!=)—ER—WHY NOT TRY A POEM, SON?

Ef Ah Had Mah Druthers
by A. Yokum, Age 18

Ah druther hold yo'
hand beneath the moon
Than bash in the haid
of Earthquake McGoon
Ah druther gaze into
yore eyes
than eat a mess of
polecat pies

Ah druther see yore
smile so sweet
Than see mah pappy
wash his feet
Ah druther waste the
whole day wif yo'
Than waste the
same wif Hairless Joe
Ah druther win yo'
fo' a prize
Than win a hawg of
equal size

To have yo' an' to
have no other
Thet is the thing Ah'd
mostly druther?
Ah'd druther jump in
the lake tomorror
                  moon
Than not get no
letter fum Lorna
Goon

writ by hand.

LI'L ABNER

by AL CAPP!!

WH-WHUT'LL AH **DO**?— AH STILL DIDN'T GIT NO ANSWER FUM LORNA GOON!!

(—**NATURALLY**!—I'M SAVING ALL HIS LETTERS, TO GIVE OUT AS PUBLICITY, AFTER HIS SUICIDE!"—) WHY NOT TELL HER HOW HER NEGLECT IS RUINING YOUR APPETITE AND MENTALITY?

Dere Lorna Goon:
Oh how yore neglect has rooned mah appy-tite an mentality.
Ah will tell yo about em in the order of thar impawtince.
Fust-mah appytite. This mawnin, fo'breckfust mammy slung a dozin poke chops to me.
Eemajine the look of anguish on her face wen she seen ah left 3 poke chops un-et!—oh, son whuffo is yo got so

bird-like a appy-tite, she moaned at me! But ah dast not tell her the **reel** reason witch is becuz yo keeps on not ritin to me.
Ef yo wishes me to die of starvay-shun, just keep on not ritin them letters yo dont send me.
Mah **mentality** is also gittin weeker witch is a crime on account of a travelling man once toed me ah was a fust class moron.

Yestiddy Fantastic Brown axed me how much was 3 plus 2. It took me a **half hour** longer than usual to calcoolate iit an even then ah had to use mah toes an fingers.
Ef these sort of things keeps on ah will probly develops into merely a Big Stoopid Hill-billy fum yore lovable
A. Yokum
moron,
fust-class.

STILL NO ANSWER FUM LORNA GOON! RECKON THAR'S NO USE WRITIN' HER NO MO', HUH, MISTAH SHAKESPEARE?— RECKON AH BETTER GO **SEE** HER, HUH?—

SEE HER?— NO! NO!! (—"IF HE ONCE LAID EYES ON THAT OLD WRECK —THE WHOLE STUNT WOULD COLLAPSE!"—)

IN A PLAY I ONCE WROTE, "**ROMEO AND JULIET**," THE LOVER PRETENDED TO **KILL** HIMSELF!!—WHY DON'T **YOU** TRY THAT?—WRITE LORNA GOON, **PLEADING** WITH HER, TO ANSWER—(—"SHE **WONT**!—I'LL SEE TO **THAT**!!"—)

TELL HER THAT IF SHE **DOESN'T** ANSWER—YOU'LL SHOOT YOURSELF THROUGH THE HEART, IN **HER** FRONT PARLOR—**ON CHRISTMAS EVE!!** NATURALLY, THE GUN WILL BE LOADED WITH **BLANKS!** (—"THEY WONT BE BLANKS— I'LL SEE TO **THAT!**"—)

HEARING THE SHOT, SHE WILL DASH MADLY FROM HER BOUDOIR, AND SOB OUT HER LOVE FOR YOU, OVER YOUR APPARENTLY DEAD BODY!! **WOMEN ARE LIKE THAT!!**

THEY **IS**, HUH? OH-**HO**! **HO**! THE **SAPS!**

Li'l ABNER

by AL CAPP!!

Dere Lorna Goon—

How many times do ah hafta tell yo' that ah is so stoopified wif love fo' yo' that ah is willin' to say yes if yo' will ax me to marry up wif yo'?

Ef yo' does not anser this letter ah will shoot mahself smack throug the hart on Chris-mus Eve in yore front parlor causin yo' to dash madly outa yore boodwar an' sob out yore love fo' me over mah carcass.

respeckfully yourn
the future late A. Yokum
age 18

(writ by hand.)

—BUT—("CHUCKLE!!")—TH' GUN'LL BE LOADED WIF BLANKS!!—WILLIAM SHAKESPEARE WILL SEE T' THET!!—OH, WE IS A COUPLE O' SLY ONES, ME AN' WILLIAM SHAKESPEARE !!!

THIS LETTER WILL ESTABLISH PROOF THAT HIS SUICIDE WAS CAUSED BY HIS HOPELESS LOVE FOR THAT OLD WRECK, LORNA GOON !! — THE WORLD'S GREATEST PUBLICITY STUNT NEARS IT'S GLORIOUS CLIMAX !!

WOLFNAGEL'S INSTRUCTIONS WERE TO WIRE UP THIS ROOM, SO THAT A CERTAIN EVENT, WHICH WILL OCCUR HERE ON CHRISTMAS EVE, WILL BE HEARD FROM COAST TO COAST — BY THE SAME AUDIENCE THAT'S WAITING TO HEAR THE PRESIDENT'S CHRISTMAS EVE MESSAGE !!

THE GREATEST AUDIENCE ON EARTH WILL ACTUALLY HEAR A HANDSOME YOUNG MAN KILL HIMSELF FOR THE LOVE OF ME !!

YOU JUST BE SURE AND STAY OUT OF HIS SIGHT—UNTIL HE'S SAFELY DEAD!

MEANWHILE: DOGPATCH—

SON! — THE TIME HAS COME TO PULL OUR SLY LITTLE STUNT ON LORNA GOON! THERE'S THE GUN WITH WHICH YOU'LL PRETEND TO KILL YOURSELF !!

BUT, HA! —HA! IT'S FULL O' BLANKS! YIPPAY!

BAM!

OH! (CHUCKLE!) HOW WE IS GONNA FOOL HER! — SOME PEOPLE IS SECH SAPS !!—

Li'L ABNER
by AL CAPP*!!*

OH, DEAR!! — I FORGOT TO TELL THE SERVANTS TO REMOVE THAT EXPENSIVE RUG! I SUPPOSE HE'LL *MESS IT UP!* —

QUIET! —EVERY WORD IS BEING BROADCAST!

—THIS SUICIDE IS COMIN' T'YO' THROUGH TH' COURTESY O' LI'L ABNER YOKUM!! DUE TO CIRCUMSTANCES BEYOND MAH CONTROL, AH IS IN LOVE OF THET *GLAMMY-RUSS STAR* O' *STAGE* AN' *SCREEN* — FAVORITE O' *MILLIONS* —

WHOSE *CHARM* AN' *BEAUTY* HAVE-UH-*CAP-TIV-AY-TED* TH' HEARTS O' MOVIE-GOERS THROUGHOUT TH' WORLD — NAMELY *YO'*-LORNA GOON!! BUT—SINCE *YO'* DON'T LOVE *ME* — AH IS SIGNIN' OFF, FO'EVAH!!

WHEN YO' HEARS TH' SHOT, IT WILL BE EXACKLY TH' TIME AH IS *DAID!!* *AH'LL BE DOWN IN A FLASH, WIF A CRASH!!*

BANG!

12-24

HE'S GONE *THIS* CHRIS'MUS—OUR SON, AN' DAISY MAE'S SWEETHEART—NAMELY LI'L ABNER!!

WAL, *WE* KNOWS HE'S SAFE —AN' IS COMIN' BACK SOON. BUT (*GULP!*) S'POSE HE WERE GONE SOMEWHAR WHAR HE *WARN'T* SAFE — SOMEWHAR HE MIGHT *NOT* COME BACK FUM!!—WHUT'D WE DO THEN?

PRAY FO' HIM, NATCHERLY!

Merry Crismus

12-25

NATCHERLY!—AN' WE C'D DO EVEN *MORE.* FO' INSTANCE, WE C'D BE *EXTRY* KIND AN' HELPFUL T' *OTHER* BOYS-BOYS WHO HADN'T WENT AWAY YET!

LIKE, FO' INSTANCE, AXIN' 'EM IN FO' DINNER!

OR FO' ME NOT T' BE STAND-OFFISH WIF 'EM, LIKE SOME GALS IS *APT* T'BE—BUT, BE FRIENDLY AN' HORSE-PITTABLE!!

RIGHT! — IN OTHER WORDS, WE GOTTA TREAT 'EM LIKE WE WANT OTHER FOLKS T' TREAT *OUR* BOYS!! *ALL* OF 'EM IS *SOMEBODY'S* BOYS-ALL OF 'EM IS FINE BOYS!!

181

And it *is* a happy day when you can get *all* the *Li'l Abner* volumes published so far— and subscribe to future volumes to boot! Kitchen Sink Press has both back volumes and subscriptions available of the *complete* reprinting of Al Capp's *Li'l Abner*. Each *Abner* book contains at least one year's worth of daily strips. You'll get complete stories and meet all the fabulous characters Al Capp created. For subscription information and a free catalog listing all our fine books, magazines and comic books, drop a card to:

Kitchen Sink Press
No. 2 Swamp Rd.
Princeton WI 54968